STICKY WICKET

Gardening in Tune
with Nature

STICKY WICKET

Gardening in Tune with Nature

PAM LEWIS

SPECIAL PHOTOGRAPHY BY
Andrew Lawson

FRANCES LINCOLN

To Peter

Frances Lincoln Limited
4 Torriano Mews
Torriano Avenue
London NW5 2RZ

Sticky Wicket: Gardening in Tune with Nature
Copyright © Frances Lincoln Limited 2005
Text copyright © Pam Lewis 2005
Photographs copyright © 2005 Pam Lewis
except jacket and pp 2-3, 5, 6, 13, 16-17, 32, 35,
37, 40, 44, 48-9, 63, 65, 86-7, 98, 109, 116,
121, 132-3, 156, 158, 163, 170-1, 198
copyright © Andrew Lawson
Illustrations copyright © Anne Wilson 2005
except plan illustration pp 14-15
copyright © Ed Brooks 2003

First Frances Lincoln edition 2005

British Library Cataloguing-in-Publication data
A catalogue record for this book is available from
the British Library

ISBN 0 7112 2480 3

Conceived, edited and designed for
Frances Lincoln Ltd by
Berry & Co (Publishing) Ltd
47 Crewys Road
Child's Hill
London NW2 2AU

Edited by Susan Berry
Design and illustrations by Anne Wilson
Plan illustration by Ed Brooks
Index by Marie Lorimer

Printed in Singapore

9 8 7 6 5 4 3 2 1

Contents

PREFACE

Sticky Wicket is primarily a wildlife garden but also a romantic and peaceful place of great character and charm. In the following chapters, I describe my inspiration and incentive, my design and planting and the link with the immediate environment and how our garden is holistically managed to be in tune with nature. By "nature" I refer to the interrelationship between the soil (which underpins all life), the garden plants and associated creatures, the aspect of the land, weather patterns, light and shade, the scent, aroma and other virtues of plants, their tactile quality and the sounds we hear. By "gardening in tune with nature" I mean understanding, respecting and working in step with all these elements so that organic garden husbandry is more logical to undertake and much more rewarding to carry out.

Human nature also has to be considered; notably our emotional responses, our inherent need for order, our desire to enhance and embellish our surroundings and our penchant for acquiring and cosseting a collection of plants. I, too, want to satisfy these human needs. I try to use my wildlife-friendly plants to paint beautiful living pictures in the garden and in the way I grow crops but without inflicting chemicals on my soil, my plants, my wildlife or myself – in fact exactly the reverse.

By adopting this holistic approach, encouraging a natural equilibrium between plants and beneficial wildlife, I can successfully manage my garden using organic methods. A finely balanced interrelationship has developed between living things, including plants and creatures, and the less evident, but crucially important fungus and bacteria. "Good guys" will prey on those that are pests to gardeners and our flowers will be pollinated to provide seed and berries for ourselves and our wildlife.

I observe, enjoy and allow myself to be guided by nature as I "nudge things along" rather than "enforce an extreme regime". The trick is to be patient, pragmatic at times, and to temper reasonable measures of control with a sympathetic and lenient attitude. The pay-back I get for my work and forbearance is enjoying the response as I watch my garden flourish artistically and simply buzz with wildlife, and being able to help and encourage others who may wish to achieve similar goals.

The principles and practices of making and managing a natural and wildlife-friendly garden can be scaled to size and applied to even the tiniest backyard which, multiplied by a potential 270,000 hectares of amassed garden wildlife oasis, signifies great hope for an enlightened future for our environment.

Pam Lewis, Sticky Wicket, January 2005

INTRODUCTION

W E CAME TO STICKY WICKET with all our possessions and animals, including a horse and several hens and ducks, stacked in a cattle truck. It was October 1986; we had moved from Hampshire to Dorset with no job, no money and no idea what we would do.

On the plus side we now had our own home with five acres of land. We also had open minds and were used to hard work and "making do". Peter and I had enjoyed a life-long, hands-on connection with the land, both as farmers and gardeners. We had loved our farming life but times were changing both in agriculture and in the countryside. Over the years, we had witnessed the destruction of so much of our natural and semi-natural wildlife habitat, for which farmers hold a large share of the blame. Giving something back to the environment seemed the right thing to do, and making a wildlife-friendly garden was our first intention. I wanted to throw all my experience, energy and artistic inclinations into making a joy and a success of this project and Peter, with his extraordinary physical strength and tenacity, would help to shape it. The five acres of grass pasture that surrounded the house were in a neglected and dejected state. There was limited appeal for wildlife and only the faintest indication that someone had, at one time, vaguely intended to make a garden. With some previous experience in designing and making gardens, Peter and I immediately focused on the ways we could change and manage our few acres efficiently. We wanted our land to become a safe haven for wildlife and, at the same time, be beautiful, creative and productive for us. All these elements were to guide our garden-making and our future in Dorset.

One writer, Chris Baines, had a very positive influence. In his excellent and inspiring book *How to Make a Wildlife Garden*, Professor Baines explains how gardeners can help to make sanctuaries for much of our displaced farmland wildlife. As the face of the countryside continues to be dramatically changed, wildlife is increasingly harassed and displaced by modern farming practice, political manipulation and building developments, and many species of flora and fauna have become victims, some even driven to extinction. Fortunately, our gardens can become a constructive part of the vital network of alternative habitat that exists in our road verges, canals and riversides, coastal regions, parks and open spaces.

There needs to be a "green corridor" system, through which the creatures and plants can move and spread from one small safe haven to another, and find shelter and sustenance along the way.

There are, of course, certain plants and creatures that cannot adapt to the sort of habitat most of us have on offer in our gardens; for instance, the green-winged orchid, the chalkhill blue butterfly and the otter all have very specific habitat requirements in order to be able to survive and breed. We have to rely on a very few dedicated individuals and conservation organizations, such as the Wildlife Trusts, to protect such rare species. However, with our garden wildlife projects we can boost the chances of survival for thousands of less exotic species which also desperately need safeguarding.

I realized that this is where our individual patches of land are so important – we can all do our bit to help and the more gardeners who do so, the less fragmented and more connected our web of wildlife corridors can become. In Britain around two and a half million acres of land are said to be cultivated as part of the fifteen millions of gardens estimated to exist. To some extent, these gardens can be made to mimic some vital natural habitats such as woodland glades, wetlands and grasslands. These mini-habitats can be made viable in just a few square yards of garden – or even on a balcony – but of course with a larger area the opportunities and chances of success are multiplied. The design of the garden, the plants we select and the way we manage our gardens are the keys to success.

A pond, of whatever size, with native water plants is a very good start and is guaranteed to generate instantly gratifying results. Trees and hedges can be planted to mimic semi-woodland type of wildlife-friendly habitat, especially if British native plants can be included. Well-sited bird-feeders, bird-baths and nesting-boxes will further boost the chances of supporting and increasing the local bird population. There is a vast selection of glamorous, ornamental garden plants and wildflowers that will appeal to bees and butterflies and other important insects, such as hoverflies and beetles, which will feed on the pollen and nectar. In return, they help pollinate our plants and some will prey on insects we regard as pests. Most of these plants need to be grown in an open but sheltered place – the natural equivalent of a sunlit woodland glade. Fruits and berries, and seeds and nuts, will feed many of our birds and some of the small mammals that most of us can most easily accommodate in our gardens. There is a wealth of both wild plants and garden plants to help in this respect. Thousands of acres of lawn consume thousands of gallons of fossil fuel and chemicals to keep them maintained with only a limited value to wildlife. A little patch of fertilizer- and herbicide-free meadow, on the other hand, can support thousands of creatures and, although some are so small as to be invisible to the naked eye, they are all vital links in the food chain for wildlife.

With all this in mind, I drafted the "grand plan" for our land and, in 1987, we began making our Frog and Bird Gardens. By then we had had time to assess the site and our immediate environment and we fully understood the nature of our fertile loam-over-clay soil, which needed to be very carefully handled. The following year we began preparations for the Round Garden, where we intended to lavish our attention on growing nectar plants to attract beneficial insects. At the same time we planted the small birch copse, the little orchard area and the great hawthorn hedge which were to eventually shelter and enfold our "sunny glade". We already had one enormous asset for wildlife: the 350m (400yd) of hedgerow that formed the boundary of our land and, amongst the wide range of native species, the five mature oaks spaced along it. In 1990 we forged on with the making of our White Garden, which was intended to be much wilder than the other gardens and would help to merge our garden discreetly into the beautiful surrounding countryside.

We spent part of the next six years consolidating our work, learning how best to apply organic methods to manage the garden sensitively, and trying to persuade our pasture and part of the White Garden to be conducive to growing wildflowers. This was altogether a different ball game! Peter and I had many years of previous experience managing grassland but the nature of our soil, with its high fertility, showed a remarkable resistance to change. This set us a challenge that was to grasp our interest, change our lives and eventually commit us to a future specializing in and dedicating ourselves to the conservation of the flora and fauna of grassland. Only after thorough research, much physical effort and hours of soul-searching did we take the plunge and scrape the topsoil from half an acre of land to make the species-rich wildflower meadow (the New Hay Meadow) adjoining the White Garden (the subject of my first book, *Making Wildflower Meadows*).

My finely prepared life-size canvas was blank before I began the systematic planting of each individual garden. We had been very thorough in the planning, design and construction of our garden before carefully preparing the soil. We were at opposite poles to the quick-fix make-over teams we so often see on television! Eventually it was time to put the paint on the canvas and begin planting. During the design stages I had begun to loosely sketch out my thoughts on planting. The major structural planting such as woodland copses, hedges and shelter belts were settled in my mind. Design and planting must run hand in hand to some extent but I find it best not to get too caught up in detailing specific plants in the early stages unless very special planting conditions are likely to be required.

I had clear ideas about which colours I wanted to use in each garden. The colours were to relate to the seasonal and ecological focus I was placing on each garden area. For instance, several of our native pond and bog plants and early spring-flowering plants are yellow so I followed their lead and used yellow as the main colour for my Frog Garden. In the Bird Garden I chose pink because I wanted an extended range of plants giving me a long season of flowering; there are pink forms and varieties of most garden plants and many of our wildflowers are pink. Insects, such as bees and butterflies, are very often attracted to plants in the blue/violet/magenta spectrum so my Round (nectar) Garden needed to include these colours. Many plants with fruit, berries and autumn colour have white flowers and there were plenty of white wildflowers that would contribute handsomely to my White Garden with its "fruit forest".

I started off in a very disciplined way before unleashing my creative inclinations. I researched my subject in great detail and made a long list of all the plants I could possibly need for a thriving wildlife garden on a neutral, loamy but heavily clay-based soil. Garden wildlife requires plants to provide a variety of both food and habitat. Food plants include those that supply nectar, pollen, fruit, nut, berry or seed and very often some leaves for the infant (larval) stage in the cycle of insect development. Useful habitat plants provide shelter from the elements and protection from predators as the creatures hunt or forage for food, court, mate and rear their young and perch, roost, hide-out, hibernate or build nests.

I also listed the plants I wanted to grow to nourish my own body and soul. I intended to continue my tradition of growing as much of my own food as can be easily produced in our home conditions. I wanted my plants to be grown "cottage-garden style" in that they would be arranged in a seemingly random mixture of edible and decorative plants seasoned with useable herbs. I most certainly yearned for a sequence of scented and aromatic plants – particularly surrounding the house.

Fragrance often triggers nostalgic memories and there were some favourite plants I needed for emotional stimulation. I am passionate about meadows so wildflowers and grasses would be a thread running through all the gardens. Although I love to pick and browse my way around the garden, I am not a bit interested in gathering quantities of plants for interior flower arranging. However, I do love to have a little "nosegay" of fresh flowers and herbs on my kitchen table and beside my bed. The lists grew longer and longer but I knew they would be rationalized because I am a composer of plants rather than a compulsive collector.

While I was mulling over the proposed composition, I found this inspiring quote by George Eliot in *Scenes from Clerical Life*, first published in 1857:

> "A charming paradisiacal mingling of all that was pleasant to the eye and good for food. You gathered a moss rose one moment and a bunch of currants the next. You were in a delicious fluctuation between the scent of jasmine and the juice of gooseberries."

She had perfectly expressed my own romantic notions.

I had brought a "Noah's Ark" of plants from my previous garden, many of which were herbs. Most of our British native plants enjoy a reputation of having herbal virtues, capable of curing any complaint from the bubonic plague and wounds inflicted by mad dogs to modern-day allergies and even some cancers. I am fascinated by herbs and astonished at the power and the potency of plants. I find it terrifying to think of a future where genetically manipulated plants will inevitably escape into the countryside and into gardens. Some may hybridize with our wild plants and potentially pollute the genetic stock of plants which, as yet unbeknownst to us, may hold health-giving or even life-saving attributes. By happy coincidence, many of the top-of-the-range insect nectar plants are herbs and they are all beautiful – lavender, rosemary, fennel, marjoram and thyme are old favourites. I was delighted by how well the interests of wildlife, wildflower gardener and herbalist neatly overlap.

Having developed my planting brief I began to dreamily compose the picture I would paint. I wanted my borders to vary in terms of rhythm and pace. The style

Undulating grasses glisten at the feet of the upstanding valerian (*Valeriana officinalis*); foxtail barley grass (*Hordeum jubatum*) and *Stipa tenuissima* are signature plants in our garden.

of some would seem to be measured and controlled – almost static and becalmed. In other places I wanted the assembled plants to wave, flow, flutter and blow or weave, tumble and thread together. I tried to foresee and capitalize on the way sunlight and shadow, wind and rain, frost and dew would contribute, casting their magical spells over the images, making them sparkle, shimmer, glisten and glow. I think these less definable qualities of planting need to evolve from a hands-on relationship with the garden and by giving the plants sufficient space and scope to express their character and charisma. Some of the most magical planting events have resulted from a smouldering idea that has "spontaneously combusted", perhaps because of the way the plants have spilled over each other or from some self-set seedlings volunteering their services. The combined design and planting is like arranging a stage set, then directing the dance choreography to the music of the sounds of the countryside: a somewhat clichéd but nevertheless descriptive comparison.

PLAN OF STICKY WICKET GARDENS

Our two-and-a-half-acre gardens are surrounded by a
further two and a half acres of varied grassland, mature,
species-rich hedgerows and small wooded areas that
provide vital natural habitat for the wildlife that visits
the garden.

1   THE FROG GARDEN

Creating ponds and wetland habitat was an urgent priority when we first set out to transform our land from neglected pasture into a flourishing wildlife haven.

2   THE BIRD GARDEN

A special focus on attracting birds close to the house and a very personal garden where we joyfully watch and welcome the ever-increasing numbers and range of visiting and resident birds.

3   THE ROUND GARDEN

A paradise for bees and butterflies and beneficial insects and an equal attraction for all who visit this sheltered, sunny glade.

4   THE WHITE GARDEN

Our white-flowered wilderness garden with its "fruit forest", grassland, woodland edge and hedgerow habitat provides for all creatures large and small.

5   THE GARDEN MEADOW

A mixture of wildflowers and naturalized garden plants grows in the fertile, loamy grassland within the garden.

6   THE NEW HAY MEADOW

An important conservation project where topsoil was removed to enable us to grow a diversity of wildflowers harvested from very few remaining local, traditional hay meadows.

7   BIRCH COPSE

Just a few birches and a couple of Scots pines were all that was needed to satisfy many species of woodland flora and fauna.

THE FROG GARDEN

The Frog Garden has predominantly spring and early-summer planting with yellow and blue colouring. The special features are the recently enlarged ponds and bogs where amphibians breed and birds drink, bathe and gather mud for nesting.

Just six months after construction, the new ponds look long-established and local wildlife is already settling in.

THERE ARE CONSIDERABLY fewer ponds left on farmland in the countryside nowadays. Some ecologists suggest, as a result, that if it were not for our garden ponds, the frog would be in danger of becoming extinct. What an alarming thought both for the frog and for the gardener, for whom he is a slug-consuming friend. The garden pond can provide a constant, local source of water for pond-life battling to exist in a particular area. Amphibians lack the mobility of birds, mammals and insects, which can easily travel many miles seeking pastures new, so if just one pond is destroyed, an entire ecosystem could be wiped out.

The reduction in farmland ponds began to occur as water became easy to pump and pipe around the countryside, and the ponds were filled in to increase further the acreage of surplus crops. There are still some woodlands (which are the best for pure water), nature reserves, disused quarries, depressions, dew ponds and village ponds, but farmland, anyway, is a hostile place for a frog. Harmful chemicals that run off agricultural land often contaminate the surviving, undrained wetlands. Frogs and other amphibians are very susceptible to harm from such chemicals, especially the toxic ones associated with the growing of maize – whether conventional or genetically modified. These chemicals run off the soil surface of fields, enter the watercourses and all too easily end up in the places frogs use as a breeding ground. Since frogs and toads cannot survive without still water in which to breed, many now seek asylum in gardens where, although not all ornamental ponds are wildlife-friendly, they often get lucky and find the right sort of unpolluted, predator-free, alternative habitat in which to spawn their young. However, they do run the gauntlet of strimmers and mowers when they settle for the comparative safety of our gardens. What a predicament!

BALANCE OF AQUATIC SPECIES   There are many other fascinating creatures that also live in water or require water during part of their life-cycle. Besides frogs, we love to see toads, newts, dragonfly nymphs, caddis larvae and water beetles. There are also native water-loving plants and marginal plants, such as yellow loosestrife and flag iris, which need a safe home. Their natural riverside habitat is being eroded by invasive alien species erroneously put on sale in garden centres. Once these escape from gardens and enter watercourses, they can block waterways and cause irresolvable problems in the countryside. Some of these greedy species, such as parrot feather (*Myriophyllum aquaticum*), floating pennywort (*Hydrocotyle ranunculoides*), water fern (*Azolla filiculoides* and *A. caroliniana*) and Australian swamp stonecrop (*Crassula helmsii*) are aquatic. Himalayan balsam (*Impatiens glandulifera*), Japanese knotweed (*Petasites japonicus*) and giant hogweed (*Heracleum mantegazzianum*) can proliferate excessively at the water's edge. The all-enveloping plants are further boosted by the chemical nutrients entering our waterways, giving them an unfair advantage over our native wildflowers, which are swallowed up by the rampant vegetation. Once there is an imbalance to plant-life, there is an automatic distortion to animal life.

How can we gardeners help? Garden pond-making is one of the most instantly gratifying wildlife projects, with a guaranteed result if the basic construction and planting guidelines are in place. Almost as soon as the project is complete, the pond dwellers miraculously gravitate to the habitat they crave. In fact, our local frogs were found loitering all around us, as if queuing up for a place, when we filled our first pond with water. The whole of this lower garden soon picked up the nickname the "Frog Garden" and the title stuck.

DESIGN

The design for this garden began with, and centred around, the desire to make a wildlife pond. We mentally positioned it where we could see it from some of the house windows and, most conveniently, at the lowest point on our property where we noticed water had a tendency to gather but not, fortunately, in depths that could make excavations complicated.

We were actually making the best of what could have been a tricky situation for most ordinary gardening. The water-logging we had experienced was as much to do with land abuse as it was land levels; previous builders' disregard for the soil strata and structure had been absolute. The worst imaginable topsoil/subsoil mix had occurred where a cesspit had once been installed and then later filled in. We had inherited a sticky, swampy, nightmare corner, but this lent itself ideally to our wetland project.

In this sheltered south-westerly corner there were good light levels so we could easily reach our aim of having one third of our pond as open, sunny water surface and two thirds of it shaded, at least for part of the day. Fortunately there were no nearby conifers (which produce an acidic run-off that pollutes water) but the nearby oak would be a mixed blessing come autumn when it shed its leaves and acorns. However, for bats and many insects the positioning would be highly appropriate and the tree would provide a little of the pond's necessary shade for part of the day.

BORDERS AND LAWNS I decided I would arrange the borders and lawn in the space left after we fixed this main feature and after siting some screening trees in strategic positions. As the ideas began to gel, I set out the design using sketch plan, thick pencil, assorted sticks and yards of yellow hose and bale-string – all very high tech! The exact position and shape of the pond, and its attendant planting area, were paramount; the rest of the design would follow logically from that starting point.

SURROUNDING HEDGES, ROADS AND WATERCOURSES I wanted my planting to integrate softly with the views of our highly valued boundary hedgerows, preserving my vista of the bustling wildlife already in residence. Because the road was so close, the sides would have to be trimmed annually but that would stimulate dense, twiggy growth as well as keeping access and vision clear along the narrow lanes.

We (and our wildlife) would be well contained and sheltered, and the thorny plants, such as blackthorn and dog rose, would help keep both the creatures and our property secure from intruders. Apart from the intermittent sound of traffic we need hardly know the road was so close. However, roads are a dreadful hazard to wildlife, especially frogs and toads that move slowly and are not the least bit streetwise. I like

With plans set for three of our four gardens, work began in 1987 as we laid out and constructed paths, pergolas and borders at the entrance to the Frog Garden.

to think they would prefer to stay at Sticky Wicket rather than be tempted to migrate away. Even though I sometimes find one or two squashed on the tarmac, I can never be sure if they were our residents leaving home or newcomers looking for a place to breed as the neighbouring gardens do not always have wildlife-friendly ponds. The River Lyden trickles by within 300 yards of the garden but frogs, toads and newts require water which is quite still and with reasonably constant depths; the river is too variable in all respects to be ideal for pond-life.

NEIGHBOURING WILDFLOWER OASIS Although a fairly busy country lane borders this garden on its north and west sides, to the east lies the village cemetery – nice quiet neighbours for us and very special extra habitat for wildlife. The graveyard is a tiny oasis of the kind of wildflowers that grew in the ancient meadowland before it was set aside as a burial place about 50 years ago. They have fortunately survived because no chemicals have ever been applied, it is mown several times a year and the cut grass always removed (which helps to prevent nutrient build-up).

OUR SMALL GRASSLAND PROJECT Inspired by what we had observed over our hedge, Peter and I wanted to make a "weedy-by-design" lawn which would become a colourful, nectar-filled and seed-rich mini-meadow. We noted that, next door, where the yellow meadow ants had worked away over the years, some of the grave mounds had slowly grown into well-drained heaps of crumbly clay and formed curious shapes (I refer to them as the "spooky humps"). The queen ant has her nest below the soil surface but the workers beaver away to make the anthills, which maintain an ambient temperature to create premium breeding conditions for her. The most delicate of wildflowers grew at the highest point of these mounds. We would use this intelligence to help us mimic suitable planting conditions with our own interpretation of these "spooky humps".

We divided our lawn into two parts: one would remain damp and fertile but, if we wanted to try to imitate the favourable conditions of the grave mounds in our garden, we would have to actively create a dry, nutrient-starved lawn feature using rubble and clay.

Like the rest of the five acres of land, the existing turf in the frog garden site was comprised of a mixture of grasses with white clover and creeping buttercup. We needed a grassy arena in the centre but certainly not one of those over-manicured, over-green, stripy jobs. I saw the potential for making my lawn interesting and useful to wildlife while also providing a play area for my three dogs in their ebullient youth, and us with the perfect place to enjoy a well-spread picnic with our friends, as I had an area of about 7 by 10m (22 by 32 yd) left after the borders and ponds had been carved out.

We intended to design all the gardens with fairly limited lawn space to minimize mowing, which is not an eco-friendly activity. Paradoxically though, even mown lawns can be very attractive for wildlife, provided they are never treated with chemicals, which we would never do. The best way forward in this situation was to make a virtue of what existed, adding more wildflowers to make a flowering lawn that would be mown for most of the year but with periods of flowering in spring and early summer. I placed a wildlife-friendly, shapely specimen tree in the corner of the lawn to provide a shade for the seat I would, in my dreams, one day set beneath the leafy canopy. The bird cherry, *Prunus padus*, turned out to be a first-class choice in all respects.

CONNECTING ONE GARDEN TO ANOTHER Although the adjoining Bird Garden was to be a separate "room", the rhythm of the design flowed from one to another, so the two were mapped out at the same time. The gentle, sensuous curves of the ponds and the borders and grassy areas of both gardens have been designed to give an illusion of depth at the points where the boundary hedge is closest to the house. I insisted on a wide path to surround the entire house, which would allow me to wander, sandal-shod, around the immediate vicinity, at any time of the year. Apart from bird-feeding, pond-watching and pot-watering, I had to allow for meeting my sudden impulses: to capture a moment on camera or rushing out for some impromptu weeding or dead-heading as the spirit moved me! The existing patio, a tacky-looking affair, was easily dismantled and reassembled to help with the necessary hard landscaping for a path-cum-terrace-cum-flight of shallow steps on the north side of the house.

PLANTING

The pond and bog planting would comprise almost entirely native plants to suit the needs of the amphibians and insects associated with water. The tangle of vegetation would provide cover for the creatures who would be competing for their place in the pond. I would need oxygenating plants and some aquatics with large surface leaves to shade the water below. Blanketweed and other algae are almost certain to be a problem in any artificially made pond so I needed to follow the best advice for minimizing such unwanted vegetation.

With our border planting, I took into account the other non-aquatic wildlife that would be attracted to the pond to bathe or drink, or would be drawn to the garden for other reasons. To coordinate the borders visually with the pond, bog planting and flowering lawn, I used yellow flowers (and some foliage) as the common denominator. Many pond plants are yellow and flower in the early part of the year: it is a wonderfully cheering colour, very much associated with springtime so I wanted to make this an essentially spring-orientated garden with a concentration of bulbs, and with some blue flowers to complement the yellows.

Grasses and grass-like plants in the borders and bog would unify with the fine grasses in the flowering lawns so the whole garden would have relaxed, coherent and natural style. I was pleased to find there are one or two beautiful ornamental yellow grasses and sedges that are closely related to our British native species.

For wildlife cover, *Cornus* would be ideal beside the pond, the leafy foliage offering a cool, shady retreat for frogs, toads and newts during the summer while the vibrant stem colour would be gloriously reflected in the inky pools in winter. Bearing in mind my office window faces the pond corner, there would be plenty of all-year-round action to distract and delight me as I struggled with the computer.

CONSTRUCTION – FIRST PHASE

We made this first, and lower-lying, pond using a flexible waterproof butyl liner. I wish I had had the confidence to puddle our own clay because we certainly had plenty of it but in this corner it was mixed with topsoil and not pure enough for puddling. There is a product that can be used as a substitute or addition to line clay ponds but we were advised this was not suitable for novice or faint-hearted pond-makes, and hadn't the nerve to gamble with the prospect of a dismal, fissure-edged hole if we failed in our endeavours. In hindsight this may have looked rather less depressing than the conspicuous butyl edges that can appear in periods of drought. However, butyl has distinct advantages over other man-made materials and, for first-time pond builders, it was probably the best choice.

POND EXCAVATION Once the pond site was approved and marked out, it took a body of four strong men (two of us were girls!) to hand-dig the (roughly) 4 sq m (4½ sq yd) hole during a weekend. The excavated clay soil was then used to reinforce the rubble bank on two sides to provide us with a level water surface.

Working with soil that seems to be three parts plasticene to one part goo has its advantages; it was easy to mould to the dips and shelves we wanted to create just below the water's edge. These anomalies would create gentle level changes, including warm shallows and ledges, for both plants and creatures. We removed any offending sharp stones or bits of root from the fashioned sides of the excavated hole to make certain the surface was entirely smooth (vital if the butyl liner was not to be punctured and the pond to then leak). We lined the base and sides with bits of old carpet, overlapping sheets of thick polythene and a layer of sand to protect the butyl sheet that we then dragged carefully into position.

To help the wildlife and pond plants feel at home, we put a thin layer of sand and finely sieved subsoil in the bottom of the pond. It is important to avoid over-fertile soil and especially any which may have traces of fertilizer or indeed any chemical. We slowly three-quarter filled the pond with a gentle trickle of water that barely disturbed the sand and soil base. The pond was fully filled only after the finishing touches were complete.

I can only describe the shape of this original pond as "irregularly square with rounded corners". It was over 60cm (2ft) deep in the centre and had sloping sides so that any visiting wildlife could easily come and go without getting trapped. The pond centre must be deep enough for aquatic wildlife to survive when the top portion of the pond freezes in winter. Ideally it should have been deeper, but we found with a small, saucer-shaped pond further excavation would have been difficult.

POND HABITAT The pond needed some "furniture" for the wildlife to find privacy, safety and asylum from each other; where subterfuge rather than speed is the criteria for survival such "hidey-holes" for escaping the enemy are essential. Several large boulders were placed both at the pond side and in the water and we laid some smooth stones of assorted sizes, like a pebble beach, near the edge. We then planted flag iris and kingcups to form small islands on the shallow shelves near the rounded corners, to help hide the liner in case our landscaping and water-technology skills failed to do the job. We could afford only a limited amount of materials for landscaping but were given a few large stone slabs, which we used to edge our approach to the pond. We laid them to overhang slightly and disguise the liner, and to create little areas of shade and protection for extra habitat. Setting them with small spaces in between helps to prevent wildlife getting trapped. As clay soil begins to settle it is difficult to prevent the stones from gradually sliding towards the water, especially if they are not quite large enough; as we had mixed-sized stone slabs, we had correspondingly mixed results as time went by.

THE SECOND POND We built our second pond some years later when we began to regret not having made a larger one in the first place. We made fewer mistakes with the second pond, the worst of which was using concrete to construct it. The passage of time revealed the truth about concrete ponds; they are prone to cracking in freezing weather and seem to provide perfect conditions for blanketweed to become a menace in warm weather. Also, concrete contains harmful chemicals that leach out into the water. In theory, this can be removed after several rinses with fresh water but this is not easy without a pump and a suitable place to dispose of the contaminated water.

However, we were full of enthusiasm when we – the same heroic team that dug the first pond – set out to excavate another with similar wildlife specifications. Design-wise, the pond was teardrop-shaped, any surplus water spilling gently into the first, lower pond. Hardly a gushing waterfall, this nevertheless made a pleasing trickle, and we installed a circulating pump so that it could be prompted at the flick of a switch.

THE BASE FOR THE SECOND POND We needed to dig a hole at least 15cm (6in) deeper and wider than the ultimate pond size to allow for the necessary thickness of the concrete. This time we set aside the clay spoil to make the grassland feature described below. Once the hired concrete mixer was in operation, it was all hands on deck – shovelling, barrowing, tamping, slapping, smoothing and moulding the

mixture onto the base of pegged-down heavy-gauge chicken wire that reinforced the structure. It is recommended that a 10cm (4in) layer of concrete is needed to minimize cracking but it is difficult to avoid being a little inconsistent in places, as the whole process is a race against time as the concrete begins to set mid-operation.

Finally, we mixed up a barrow-load of concrete with a few buckets of coir to make a reasonably attractive tufa-style rim to the pond and peppered it here and there with round stones that Peter had spent many hours picking out of the path gravel. We set groups of substantial-sized rocks at strategic points to make varied habitats in the pond. I can't remember how many days we left it draped in polythene to allow the concrete to set but it seemed ages to me – the most childlike member of the construction team, who couldn't wait to see the job prettied up with plants. Even when we eventually filled the pond, and could see that it looked good, we still had to wait a couple of weeks while emptying and refilling the pond twice more to remove the toxic chemicals that leach into the water from the cement. Six weeks later it was deemed habitable and the covers removed to allow creatures to begin to colonize.

ALL ABOUT WATER As tap water can exacerbate the growth of problem weed, such as blanketweed, and it may contain chemicals that are not good news for wildlife,

Shaping and excavating the site for the concrete pond was a messy and inevitably disruptive exercise but nature is very forgiving and, in the blink of an eye, the pond soon looked glorious and brimmed with pond life.

we channelled rainwater off the house to top up the pond (also helping to conserve water). A wooden barrel acts as a water butt, storing several gallons before the surplus cascades down the sides to a soakaway, from which it is piped to the pond. Admittedly, in long spells of dry weather we have to run tap water into the butt to supplement the supply but at least our input is diluted with the stored rainwater and used only in emergencies. On high days and holidays we switch on the pump which circulates and aerates water whilst yielding a pleasant sound.

We are currently researching the use of solar power, as an environmentally advantageous form of resourcing energy. I feel sufficiently confident to scribble a conspicuous note on our Christmas list alongside the request for the solar lights I have been wanting for some time. I have not yet been able to discover whether the advertised floating globes would be efficient in keeping an ice-free breathing hole for aquatic wildlife during a freeze. It would save me having to fiddle about with bowls of hot water to melt the ice (cracking it can be traumatic for underwater creatures).

POND GARDEN FEATURES

There was only one "garden feature" at Sticky Wicket when we came. The former owner had built what could be loosely described as a patio – a conspicuous square platform of slabs protruding from a doorway with four rounded, coniferous blobs at the edges. You needed to be either seven foot tall or an athlete to get on and off the "patio" without straining some part of your anatomy. We re-homed the conifers (far away in another county!) but recycled the paving as part of the construction of the wide path-cum-terrace along this north side of the house. We also reused the paving to make a flight of shallow steps to abolish the need for the death-defying leap onto the lawn. The paving slabs were at first rather grim, but reset in gravel with creeping plants threaded in and out of the patchwork, they have gradually begun to mellow. Cobbled sets would have been a preferred option but were way beyond our budget.

Recycling was an essential part of the brief for our low-cost garden-making, but I promised myself I would one day revamp some of the economy landscaping once the priority wildlife initiatives were up and running. In the meantime we saved a pile of stones from the builders' rubble dug out of the proposed planting areas. We managed to beg, steal or borrow a few more to build some dry-stone retaining walls, which formed part of the restructured terrace. As dry-stone walls are built without mortar they have lots of useful crevices for all kinds of wildlife to occupy. The skill in building such a wall is to have a good eye for exactly the right size and shape of stone to fit securely beside its neighbour. As an amateur dry-stone wall builder I am only average, but Peter revealed a superior skill and practised eye that way outshone mine.

THE SPOOKY HUMP   We were diligent in making our planting preparations suitable for extremes of both wet and dry conditions. More stone was needed on the upper edge of the Frog Garden lawn where we constructed our triangular patch, known as the "spooky hump" (see page 21). It is really just a gentle mound

We constantly explore different ways to persuade a diversity of wildflowers to grow in the varied conditions required for them to cohabit alongside selected native grasses. The "spooky hump" is designed and constructed to mimic the very special grassland habitat in our neighbouring graveyard.

but produces a sufficient micro-environment to create the well-drained and impoverished conditions that many wildflowers favour. Most fortuitously, one of our neighbours offered us some assorted rubble from his building demolition. Rubble is always a useful component of many a wildlife feature and we happily accepted. We first laid a tough horticultural fabric over the fertile soil at the base of our proposed artificial, over-sized "anthill" to form a barrier and prevent nutrients being taken up by deeper-rooted plants. Then we piled rubble on top – larger pieces first, then those of a finer grade mixed with some of the clay saved from pond excavations. To level it off, we capped it with about an inch of limestone chippings and sand. We laid a patchwork of irregularly shaped pieces of ryegrass-free turf with gaps between each – like a chequerboard. From our store of mixed wildflower seed harvested from our local churchyard we propagated about fifty plants, setting most of these into the gaps and some actually into the patchwork pieces of turf. Then we scattered the rest of the seed very finely over the whole area, crossed our fingers, and hoped for the best!

Within months our own "spooky hump" became a great joy to behold. It now helps conserve the local flora while attracting legions of insects and invertebrates, which, in turn, help to feed birds and sometimes a visiting fox or hedgehog. How wonderful it would be if the green woodpeckers that visit these humps in the neighbouring churchyard in search of ants also visit our own.

Sadly, these extremely special grave mounds and anthills were perceived as "untidy" by the parish council, and have recently been removed or tampered with, thus desecrating the locally distinct landmark and impacting on the ecosystem. Our personal quest to conserve the wildflowers became more urgent. We realized the ecological importance of these grave mounds and knew that we cannot possibly recreate such a phenomenon that has taken decades to evolve. We could, however, address the lack of awareness in our local countryside and resolved to do our best to compensate for any indifferent stewardship that contributes to the demise of Britain's wild plants and interdependent wildlife.

CONSTRUCTION – PHASE TWO

By October 2003, our original butyl pond – then 17 years old – was leaking and so overgrown it was hardly visible. It was still very much the domain of our frog population so we thought long and hard when contemplating a third, much larger, pond for our wildlife that seemed to be outgrowing the two we had. The disruption would inevitably be a bit traumatic for all the creatures in the vicinity but before we started, we carefully rescued all the pond life we could find. Many creatures were given temporary lodgings in large plastic tubs, along with some of the pond sludge and vegetation. The very few frogs in residence at the time were persuaded to visit other parts of the garden. It was some way off their breeding time and we were determined to have the pond ready before they needed to hibernate (around October) or spawn (beginning in February).

PETER'S PONDS   Peter took command of this project. There were to be no half measures this time. In spite of all the careful overall planning of the gardens, I must be honest and admit that, in our enthusiasm, we rushed into our first pond project without sufficient forethought and made mistakes. In the first place, we should have allocated a larger space for the pond, preferably further away from the nearby oak. It is not close enough to harm the tree or for the tree to cast too much shade on the pond, but the leaf-fall causes a build-up and overload of silt. Secondly, we should have considered more thoroughly the feats of water engineering needed to supply the pond with rainwater channelled from our herringbone land-drainage system. However, we were daunted by the logistics of seasonal "feast or famine" rainwater supplies. It was too technically challenging to deal with the surplus water pouring off our land during the increasingly wet winters, nor could we begin to evaluate the quantities of water that might flood in or how to deflect the surplus back into the particular watercourse we could officially access. We would just have to top up the pond with tap water in dry weather although we recognized this resolution was not ideal.

This time around Peter designed, excavated and constructed not one but two large ponds to replace the single original small one. Why two? Well, in terms of biodiversity, a series of ponds with varied habitats is more valuable than one large body of water. In our case it was also to do with land levels, the reinforcement of the sides and aspects of water engineering that left me perplexed and unable to visualize. I was grateful to be a passenger in this, and to marvel at Peter's ingenuity.

Peter applied the same successful construction principles to the new ponds as he had to the original but, with the size of this one at least tenfold the original, there was far more scope for a greater depth of water and more varied shelves and bog areas. The increased size and depth would eventually help regulate fluctuations in temperature but brought with it technical hitches when it came to making the water levels precise and when finishing the edges and disguising the liner. At each stage of the construction he used a plank and spirit level to check the levels in both directions.

He used a tufa mix for the edging about half-way around each pond. This tufa mix was made using the same combination of ingredients as before (see page 26) but with one difference. We wanted to avoid using peat and even imported coir is not really ecologically friendly. Peter used organic peat-free compost instead. It seemed a good substitute and the

Peter's ambition was to enlarge our wetland habitat from the original small ponds. He pauses momentarily while installing the pond liner during one of the construction stages in this major project.

dark colour resulted in a mix that looked like baked mud. With its reasonably organic and unobtrusive appearance, it held the edge of the liner secure and helped to protect the potentially exposed parts of the butyl from the ultra-violet rays of the sun as and when the tide-line fluctuated in dry weather. Random groups of stones, logs and both pond and marginal plants distracted from the rim-like appearance. Of the remaining edges, some were turfed and some paved as with the previous ponds. Peter also made a small bog by sinking part of the butyl lining and back-filling with soil, retained by a dam of sandbags.

Peter entrusted me with the habitat creation part of the project once his construction work was nearing completion. The large pile of leftover assorted stones waiting in the wings were randomly shaped, so to avoid the risk of leaks or damage to the liner we used mats of additional butyl, saved from the trimmings, underneath them. They were held down with small hessian bags of sand and soil into which we anchored some oxygenating plants.

More dragonflies than ever before visited the garden while our pond's progress was hurried along to beat the advancing wet winter weather. How frustrating it must have been for them to find preparations still incomplete for what promised to be a superbly safe breeding ground! For the robins, chaffinches and grey wagtails, however, the amenities were immediately usable and they were bathing in it even while work went on. Within days the frogs were back, too, and Peter was never short of wildlife company as he worked on resolving the edges. Even though we were now in October, I was unable to resist a dip before it became sacrosanct for wildlife. Peter could not believe his eyes when, on a sudden impulse, I dived into the pond fully clothed: "More like wild wife than wildlife", was his only comment. Tongue slightly in cheek, we buried a time capsule at the pond edge to remind or inform future archaeologists of our good intentions and our antics!

THE PLANTING

My first priority was to introduce some oxygenators to the muddy bottom of the pond. Water starwort (*Callitriche* sp.), spiked water milfoil (*Myriophyllum spicatum*), hornwort (*Ceratophyllum demersum*), and curly pondweed (*Tamogeton cripsus*) are recommended natives that root into the mud and improve the health of the water. I used hessian bags of sand and soil to start some of the plants going and anchor them at the appropriate depth. They multiply at a great rate and provide food and hiding places for tiny creatures.

Next I put in some plants with leaves that would float on the water surface and help reduce the light levels: The fringed water lily (*Nymphoides peltata*) is free-floating and therefore not fussy about water depths, making it ideal for any dimension of pond. With an ability to spread very rapidly, it is efficient in making a dark covering to exclude sunlight and so hamper the spread of blanketweed. In our situation, it also has the advantage of having delicate yellow flowers and small leaves that are perfectly in scale with the size of the little pond. However, for the large new ponds I have cautiously introduced the large yellow native water lily (*Nymphaea lutea*) that has much bolder flowers and leaves. I have also included broad-leaved pondweed (*Potamogeton natans*) with its olive-green oval leaves, which also lie on the surface.

The sun sets over Peter's pond, creating a serene view from our house as a community of native plants and wildlife rapidly become established during the first year.

Greater spearwort (*Ranunculus lingua*) has long, horizontal, underwater shoots with large spear-shaped leaves and huge buttercup-like flowers. It is one of the most invasive of my selection but I love it and the excess plants are easily weeded out to make good compost fodder. The bog bean (*Menyanthes trifoliata*) has leaves like a broad bean and delightful white flowers while burr reed (*Sparganium erectum*) has contrastingly sword-like leaves and globe-shaped fruits with seeds that some birds enjoy. Whether I wanted it or not, duckweed (*Lemna minor*) spread from pond to pond. The tiny, bright green leaves multiply like crazy and are a bit of a menace, but they redeem themselves by using up nutrients and helping to shade the water. To relieve the pond of a surplus, I net the excess and compost it or feed it to my very appreciative ducks.

POND MARGINS Most of my marginal plants are British natives and it is interesting how many of them are yellow. There are just a few blue ones to help unite my selected colour arrangement. At the edges of the butyl-lined ponds, at various depths of mud and water, I grow flag iris, kingcups, water-mint, water forget-me-not, and brooklime and creeping Jenny, which will both grow in the water as well as in fairly dry conditions. The damp, clay soil is ideal for yellow loosestrife, meadow buttercups, lesser spearwort, silverweed, yellow archangel and bugle. I have allowed just a few non-native plants to join the throng. Among them are: *Mimulus guttatus*, *Primula florindae*, *Iris sibirica* and a very special geranium I have named Geranium 'Blue Shimmer'. This is a beautiful and dynamic Sticky Wicket seedling that I selected for propagation. It is the progeny of our native meadow crane's-bill (*Geranium pratense*). Just for fun I added *Juncus effusus* f. *spiralis*, a crazy-looking relative of our native soft rush.

Rosebay willowherb and purple loosestrife set seed nearby and although they are somewhat at odds with the colour scheme, they are excellent for wildlife. I find them so beautiful that I eventually weakened and gave up any serious attempt to remove them. I do, however, attempt to confine them and at least regulate their spread by cutting off their seeding heads.

I had a useful idea for disguising the butyl edges. I stacked up a pile of turf removed during the excavations, covered them in black plastic and left them in the heap for about a month until the grass had been killed off but before the fibrous root

Shafts of sunlight strike the foliage of the variegated flag iris, accentuating the form of the swordlike leaves mirrored in the inky darkness of the clear water.

system had totally decomposed, so they could be easily handled. I laid them out and planted their undersides with the roots of ground-cover plants, such as periwinkle, creeping Jenny, brooklime and lamium, before draping them gently along the pond edges with an inch or so dangling into the water (making sure the turf sloped gently downwards towards the pond, to avoid drawing too much water out). This made a good job of hiding the liner and gave us a pleasing green edge that needed no mowing or strimming – operations best avoided near frogs and toads.

SHADE AND GROUND COVER Our young frogs and baby toads now benefit from the shady protection of the several varieties of cornus which grow well in the heavy clay soil turned up by the excavations. In winter we enjoy their vibrantly coloured stems. The cornuses are carpeted with Russian comfrey, which forms an immensely effective weed-suppressing ground cover that is abuzz with nectar-hungry bumble-bees in spring. The comfrey grows willingly on the sticky clay and actually helps to break chunks of it down into an almost crumbly tilth. The price I pay for growing such a useful plant is the struggle to control its advance into neighbouring plants. As I could not win in all ways, I accepted that my choice of additional planting would be limited. The silver variegated *Lamium galeobdolon*, whose yellow flowers provide a good early source of nectar, competes fairly gallantly beside the comfrey.

Years ago I made the unfortunate mistake of planting lyme grass (*Leymus arenarius*) too close to the edge of the liner. I doubt if there is, in fact, a safe distance for it. During its first summer it forged its way several feet towards the pond; its powerful underground stems managed to creep under the butyl liner and lurk there, unnoticed, until the following spring. At the first sniff of warm weather, it emerged triumphantly, the virulent strength of its new shoots piercing the liner and creating a leak, which has remained a17-year-long thorn in the side of the plantswoman who underestimated its power! I have now learned my lesson and avoid growing such furtively creeping plants – or at least within a good stone's throw of a pond.

GARDEN BORDERS

I wanted the planting on the northern boundary to be "fuzzy" – in other words, devoid of any plants with a distinctive form to achieve my intention of softly blending the garden into its surroundings. A densely wooded patch in our

neighbour's mature garden made the perfect background for our conspicuously new one. I wanted to echo the quiet look of our immediate borrowed landscape and a non-confrontational planting style would give the appearance that our land extended further into the distance. In the same respect I also wanted a stretch of mown grass between the house and this boundary to maximize the existing space and enhance this impression of distance.

"FUZZY" PLANTS Bearing in mind my yellow and blue colour scheme, I wanted an early-flowering shrub in the background of the "fuzzy border". My choice of forthysia may seem odd as most are glaringly conspicuous. However, I planted a very pale-coloured, sparsely-flowered, dark-stemmed variety called *Forsythia suspensa* f. *atrocaulis* with *Clematis alpina* as a nearby companion and a mist of forget-me-nots as

The strong form of the mature yellow borders and the tapering gravel and grass paths make the entrance to the Frog Garden inviting. As you pass through, Peter's ponds (see page 30) are revealed among the more naturalistic planting background.

ground cover. The combination was very easy on the human eye and an attraction for the early bees. The summer flowers include the soft-yellow, scabious-like *Cephalaria gigantea*, fennel and *Nepeta govaniana* with *Deschampsia cespitosa* 'Golden Veil' to make the border seem even more hazy.

This was all very satisfactory until an uninvited *Clematis montana* hijacked the hedgerow and tried to spread its curtain of growth over the border. You may wonder why I allowed this to happen to a precious native hedge. Well, beguiled by the waft of the vanilla-scented flowers, I began to weaken. In what seemed like the blink of an eyelid, the opportunist invader infiltrated the hedgerow and set its sights on scaling the oak tree, which was just when the first pair of thrushes chose to nest in the mounting tangle. No nature-loving gardener could dream of interfering with thrush habitat, certainly not me! Pruning time was at odds with nesting time, the thrushes won and the clematis rampaged out of bounds.

YELLOW AND BLUE BORDERS With a preponderance of yellow flowers adorning the ponds and borders, the relaxing blues of herbaceous plants such as *Campanula latiloba* and *C. lactiflora* and our home-bred *Geranium* 'Blue Shimmer' make a welcome contrast. This combination of colours always looks both fresh and calming. At the same time, yellow has a notably "uplifting" effect, which is particularly cheering at springtime when the countryside first comes alive with primroses, cowslips, dandelions, wild daffodils and celandines in the hedgerows. When it comes to working with colour, as in all things, I like to take my lead from nature.

SCENTED AND AROMATIC SHRUBS The gardens are all sweetened and spiced with fragrant and aromatic plants, especially in the borders closest to the house. The honey-scented *Euphorbia mellifera* appears to be dripping with nectar, but I am surprised to find little obvious reaction from wildlife, though perhaps I could watch more attentively. Some of the early-flowering shrubs, such as *Mahonia japonica* and the flower-smothered broom (*Cytisus x praecox*), are blessed with an ample supply of nectar which the queen bumblebees need for vital sustenance to start a new brood. Both shrubs fill the late-winter/early-spring air with scent and the mahonias provide summer berries (edible, but best left for the birds). I can also tap into the stimulating aroma of rosemary, santolina, sage, or bay anytime I care to brush past or pick a sprig or two from these aromatics, which flank my well-trodden routes around the garden.

Wildflowers, herbs and ornamental garden plants mingle in a relaxed way that characterizes our planting style. Cowslips, tulips and fennel cohabit charmingly while satisfying the needs of many beneficial insects.

BULBS Spring bulbs are a feature of the Frog Garden borders. I have taken some old-fashioned narcissus under my wing, caring for the shy-looking and rather unimposing varieties which I find in some of the very old gardens I manage. These natural and modest-looking narcissus seem to have been superseded by some oversized, over-coloured and downright peculiar newcomers, many of which appear to have been bred to shine on the show bench. They look embarrassed in the garden and confound the nectar-seeking bees. Of course, there are some very lovely modern varieties as well. Far and away my favourite of these is *Narcissus* 'Jenny'. She has a grace and elegance of shape that reminds me of my whippets.

There are also other bulbs, such as aconites, 'West Point' tulips, grape hyacinths and some yellow and blue crocuses which grow among my fresh, limy-green grasses and sedges (*Milium effusum* 'Aureum' and *Carex elata* 'Aurea', for example), and other delectable foliage plants, such as *Physocarpus* 'Dart's Gold'. The golden hop twines through the yellow-berried *Cotoneaster salicifolius* 'Rothschildianus' and *Viburnum opulus* 'Aureum' then rambles on into the hedgerow, scaling field maple, hazel, hawthorn and blackthorn.

Hops are the most favoured food plant of the beautiful Comma butterfly. They are said to accept the golden form so I hope they find breeding conditions suitable here.

FREE-RANGING HERBS Self-seeding herbs, such as evening primrose and fennel, are welcome to squat where they will, since they attract and feed moths and other

pollinating insects. Herbs are not confined to a regulation "herb garden" here at Sticky Wicket. They are set free among the borders and encouraged to self-seed in a fairly random way. However, allowing the entry of ginger mint was a serious mistake. Although its colouring is absolutely perfect, it has become much too headstrong and is terrorizing other species with its rampaging root system. I ferociously drag out as much as I can once a year, accept that it has the better of me and we muddle along as best we can. At least it is efficient ground cover and the bees and hoverflies like it.

WILDFLOWER VERSUS WEED   It is interesting how we call our native plants "wildflowers" when we like them and "weeds" when we don't. I grow and try to love both (almost) equally. The harebell must be one of the most beautiful, delicate and well-loved of our wildflowers. Some have seeded in my pots to make a perfect marriage of colour and form with the bell-shaped flowers of the more muscular agapanthus – a South African guest. Gardeners usually regard wildflowers such as nipplewort and greater celandine as weeds, but they are reasonably non-aggressive,

Ornamental and wild grasses, such as *Molinia variegata* and *Deschampsia cespitosa*, soften the pond edges, modestly supporting the yellow colour theme and integrating with native rushes and sedges.

quite pretty and good for wildlife, so I let some of them join the throng of other yellow flowers, provided they do not trespass too heavily on my hospitality. Greater celandine is quite different from its pesky relative, lesser celandine, which can become a weed in the fullest sense of the word when it invades a border, although I happily let it grow in my lawn. Cowslips and primroses, being far more restrained and domesticated self-seed in the borders and in the flowering lawns.

YELLOWS AND YELLOWS All the yellows I have so far mentioned are what you might call "full on", not necessarily harsh or too much on the side of chrome but, well, yellow. I have a collection of more subtly coloured plants that share their yellowness with the amber or brown overtones that I like to combine for a more painterly composition. The part of the border that greets me at my entrance gate needs to be a gentle transition from the countryside beyond, so the yellows are more subdued and the foliage colour understated.

THE BROWNISH BIAS Corokia cotoneaster, sometimes called the wire-netting plant, has tiny brown-bronze leaves on wiry, zigzag stems with minuscule yellow flowers, rather like mimosa. *Muehlenbeckia complexa* is similar in foliage but rather too adventurous in habit for those who need sanity in the border. As a sharp contrast in foliage size, *Actinidia deliciosa* has huge, leathery leaves that hide its creamy beige-yellow flowers. It makes yards of growth and anchors its thick, knobbly tan stems with conspicuous winding tendrils. The fine, tall, grassy leaves of *Chionochloa rubra* make an extreme contrast of form, but the colours include those of the aforementioned shrubs and, on close examination, extend the range to subdued orange, olive-green and buff. This quietly understated grass draws my attention and admiration all year round and, as a bonus, has a fountain of sprays of oaten flowers in summer. The grass is a match made in heaven for the unique colouring of *Diervilla sessilifolia* with its young foliage which, if you mixed its colours in a paint-box, would contain pale olive-green and an apricot blend. It has pale yellow flowers which in no way vie for attention.

SOFT, TINTED YELLOWS   Spires of yellow foxgloves punctuate the foliage composition. *Digitalis grandiflora* has a soft colouring, gentled by a hint of dull apricot, which makes it a perfect companion for the group I have described. The colours have a similar gentle hint-of-a-tint to those of *Buddleia x weyeriana* and also to the divinely perfumed *Lonicera periclymenum* 'Graham Thomas'. The strangely scented *Rosa* 'Maigold' and the more discreet *Polemonium pauciflorum* also fit well amongst these assembled plants, which all have amber tones in their various flower parts.

SPECIFIC HABITAT BOOSTERS

It is incredible how, given the right conditions, wildlife soon finds its way to a new garden habitat. Adult amphibians have a strong homing instinct so it is cruel to import them as adults, but it is permissible (although frowned upon by some ecologists) to transfer spawn, especially where it is rescued from a pond with tadpole-fancying goldfish. (There is, however, a danger of spreading a very unfortunate and little understood wasting disease called 'red leg' that is affecting frogs in many parts of the country.) Fortunately, for us, our frogs arrived of their own accord.

We certainly did not want to add fish, which compete for food and gobble up the aquatic life we sought to conserve. The only imported pond wildlife were pond snails from a friend's pond. They make a marvellous job of helping to keep the pond clean and free of excessive weed.

AQUATIC WILDLIFE   Pond skaters and water boatmen were the first pond-dwellers to move in; the former skimming the surface and the latter scudding around just below it. Heaven knows where they came from but our ponds were barely filled before they started to arrive. Whether by mutual agreement or as a result of ferocious contest, the butyl ponds are used by scores of frogs and sometimes toads, while the concrete one is occupied predominantly by newts and/or dragonfly larvae. Frogs and toads lay a massive amount of spawn to compensate for the vast

Lonicera 'Graham Thomas' provides a sweet fragrance for the rustic arbour, which is set among the softly tinted yellow flowers and foliage of the border. The seat and arbour are made from locally coppiced hazel.

quantity eaten by other creatures. Toads contribute to the health of the pond by eating decaying plants and algal growth. They hatch two weeks after the frogs and it is five years before they become sexually active adults; hence the importance of a safe, damp, shaded, muddy habitat where they can grow and survive to maturity. Dragonfly larvae, diving beetles and water scorpions gobble up a huge proportion of the pond community. I tend to champion the less tyrannical newts, which consume the larvae of mosquitoes and other undesirables when in the water and insect pests when in the garden. Of course, I have no control in the matter; I get what I am given. Some years we have a good newt season and see both common and palmate types; it seems to be swings and roundabouts when it comes to claiming and defending domains.

LOG AND STONE HEAPS   While Peter slaved away at the finer details of the landscaping, I began the fun part of the construction. At the water's edge, I piled

small stacks of logs from a range of native trees. Yearling newts particularly appreciate damp logs so the wood was deliberately gathered in varied states of decomposition. A hollow elm log had for years served as a seat by the back door but in its ancient crumbling state became an ideal woody cavern for toads or frogs. Some lengths of wood were then partly submerged for extra wildlife appeal. I make it all sound as casual as it was intended to look, but in fact each piece of wood was selected as carefully as if my composition were a possible entry for the Turner prize.

I heaped groups of large stones beside the pond and tried to avoid them looking like a third-rate rockery. Being swamped with billowing meadow crane's-bills and sedges soon took care of that. We hoped both frogs and toads would appreciate our specially constructed stone "frogarium" and "Toad Hall" – mini-caves made out of flat slabs of stone – and other built-in nooks and crannies that simulate the small, cool, damp cavities and hollows where they might naturally shelter or hibernate. I also submerged some rocky hideouts and hibernation places in the new ponds. First I gently lowered in a couple of hollow breeze-blocks and then randomly surrounded them with air-bricks and rocks, creating crevices and hollows of varied dimensions. I settled these piles with some subsoil and disguised the rather ordinary materials with some attractive stones. One such pile formed an island and the other formed a promontory from the water's edge. The frogs came to their new home in droves.

ATTRACTING OTHER WILDLIFE Hedgehogs are delightful creatures that very helpfully consume slugs as part of their varied diet. I have often seen these prickly characters in the garden but neither of us have ever actually witnessed one visit the pond to drink, although we like to think they do. Judging by the numbers that come to grief in our modern world, hedgehogs are either very unlucky or they have suicidal tendencies. They are very good at falling into ponds with steep sides, which make escape impossible for them – another good reason to make sure at least some of the pond edges are gently graded so they can drink easily or crawl to safety.

Placed at the water's edge, my carefully selected and composed "eco-heap" of mixed logs is perfect habitat for insects and young newts. The pebble-edged concrete pond is filled with fringed water-lily foliage to help suppress the growth of blanketweed, while the outer fringe of *Molinia caerulea* 'Variegata' is peppered with self-seeding mimulus.

INSECTS AND INSECT PREDATORS Bats are another creature of the night that I rarely encounter. I know we are visited by them but I see no evidence of a roost on our property, although I believe they inhabit our oak trees. Or maybe they live in my neighbours' buildings and fly in, just as our swallows do, for a gourmet feast on the insects that fly around the pond.

HOSTAS AND SLUGS I find hostas rather too solid and "static" for my liking but there are one or two places where these qualities are appropriate. I quite like to grow *Hosta* 'Honeybells' by the pond, where my population of frogs and toads help me to deal with the slug problems associated with these plants. Hostas are martyrs even more to snails, and the thrushes help here, using the stone pond surround as an anvil. We hear the tap-tapping, and see the crushed shells, evidence of their welcome feast and our much-valued organic pest control. I'd much rather see a thrush in the garden than a perfect hosta! The hostas lure the snails away from other plants and I know just where to find them. There is no question of using chemical slug control in our garden, since any poisoned creature can become food for another and the toxins get passed into the intestines of the innocent bystander; often the natural predator that would have dealt with the problem. . . had it lived.

VISITING BIRDS Apart from the underwater-dwellers and nocturnal individuals, there are other more easily discernible creatures. Our birds are predictable pondside visitors and it is a great joy to watch them bathing in the shallows and splashing water over the nearby marginal plants. Thrushes, blackbirds and starlings take their turn to bathe and drink. Pigeons drink in a very distinctive manner; both collared

Several species of visiting and resident birds like to drink and bathe in the stony shallows of the small concrete pond and thrushes use the larger stones as an anvil for cracking snail shells.

doves and wood pigeons suck up water as if they were drinking through a straw and give the impression they are getting immense relief from a burning thirst. When they treat their "bar" as a washing facility, they extract yet more water using their amazingly strong wings to splash a cascade over the edges.

It is quite hard to leave bare, wet earth for swallows, martins and other birds to use for nest building. Every patch of earth soon becomes colonized with vegetation, but I suspect the birds are astute at spotting nesting materials without my thinking I must leave glaringly obvious mud-flats to help. After all, when your property has previously been christened Sticky Wicket, there is plenty of sludgy ground around, especially where horses and chickens have scraped and scratched bare patches.

IN CONCLUSION

We learned a great deal as we met the challenges of pond making and can honestly say that this project has been a huge success story in terms of the pleasure we have received, the beauty we see and in constructing a truly important wildlife and wild plant conservation resource. The more gardeners who make wildlife-friendly ponds, the greater the chances of survival for our poor wetland refugees. Whether the pond is the size of a lake or just a washing-up bowl, results are guaranteed to be rapid and encouraging, providing hours of lively entertainment watching the constant buzz of wildlife activity in and around the water and surrounding planting.

So far we have had a pond unfailingly crammed with frogs at mating and spawning time in February, when the resonance of croaky frog-song is quite astonishing. I was determined not to be put off by Peter's comment that this strange cacophany sounded like "the reverberation of a submerged moped" – a typically unromantic, male interpretation of a unique sound – but an accurate description, nonetheless!

THE BIRD GARDEN

In our Bird Garden the focus is on providing features, many of them hand crafted, to attract birds so that they can best be viewed from the house. The pink and plum-coloured plants in this part of the garden provide a long season of attractive flowers and foliage.

A home-made bird-bath, set into a carpet of nectar-rich plants and grasses, provides the centrepiece for this area.

A S WITH ALL OUR BRITISH WILDLIFE, birds are having a tough time living in 2lst-century Britain. Numbers of some species are in steep decline; the population of thrushes and skylarks, for example, has halved in the last twenty-five to thirty years. Much of this misery is attributable to the extensive and excessive use of agricultural and horticultural chemicals, particularly pesticides and herbicides. They eradicate all but the most persistent insects and weeds, and in doing so remove the birds' natural food supply. Added to this, the ever-diminishing areas of natural habitat left for wildlife and pockets of unspoilt woodland, grassland and wetland are becoming increasingly isolated as more – and larger – roads scar our landscape and building developments gobble up the remaining green space.

Mile upon mile of hedgerows is ripped out every year and many that survive are ill-managed. Now that 40 per cent has been removed, every single stretch of hedgerow becomes incredibly precious – particularly those that are older and more species-rich. There is some welcome and positive work being done by conservation organizations, but I believe much tighter legislation is required to prevent this increasingly widespread harm. It is apparently illegal to destroy a bird's nest and there is a fine of up to £5,000 for doing so: yet there is no law to prevent farmers from trimming or cutting and laying hedges at bird-nesting time and thereby causing disruption or devastation. An exposed nest is a nest that is wide open to predators and therefore just as doomed as one that has actually been flailed to bits.

Gardens provide a useful habitat for at least 20 per cent of the country's populations of house sparrows, starlings, greenfinches, blackbirds and song thrushes, all of which are declining across the UK. The Royal Society for the Protection of Birds (RSPB) reckons that over 50 million birds a year become prey to cats, with house sparrows, blue tits, blackbirds and starlings being the most frequently caught. This is a disturbing figure but cats apparently thin out the weaker or sickly garden birds before they die of natural causes and the RSPB does not regard cats as the greater threat to the bird population UK-wide. They attribute the declines to habitat change and loss.

There are many wonderful breeds and groups of birds which need very specific surroundings – wading birds are an obvious example. Our garden habitat is clearly no substitute for the estuaries, mud-flats and reed beds that such birds need, nor is it likely to be suitable for some of the birds which belong in forests. It is fortunate that there remain many species with less exacting requirements, and these have adapted well to our garden environment. For instance, robins and blackbirds were originally shy, woodland birds but they now seem perfectly at home among our lawns and borders. Even rarer and more habitat-specific species (such as reed bunting) are reported to be venturing into some gardens and parks. There are many ways of encouraging birds to the garden, a wealth of plants to feed and support them, and several measures we can take to protect their welfare. Isn't it heartening to think that we gardeners are so well placed to help conserve many of our songbirds?

We are fortunate here in Dorset that there are many mature oaks in our vicinity; that a river rises just a mile up the valley and there is both dry chalk and wet clay grassland as well as wooded hills within a mile radius. Some of the visiting birds, or those which pass overhead, are there because of the features of the landscape which immediately surrounds us, and it is possible to echo some of them in microcosm using elements of design in the garden.

Several of the gardens in our village remain pretty, unspoilt cottage gardens with good hedgerows and mature trees. Sadly, others are becoming increasingly suburbanized and are no longer even faintly sympathetic to their natural surroundings. New "low maintenance" gardens, with a minimalist approach to planting may be fine for the busy householders, but they make distinctly barren places for birds and other wildlife. However, by far the most distressing consequences are wrought by the "slash and burn merchants", who move into old properties and proceed to destroy hedges and valuable cover – even during nesting periods. It is so sad when this happens because it has an inevitable knock-on effect on the wildlife in all the surrounding gardens. We need at least to fight back and explore all the ways in which we can help to compensate.

Our allocated "Bird Garden" site was approximately 5 by 9 m (15 by 18 yd) square and our design, special features and choice of plants were planned to draw in a wide range of birds and maximize our pleasure in watching them prosper. I try not to drive a wedge between the "art" and the "science" of wildlife gardening, or "gardening in tune with nature", as I call my style of design and gardening methods. In this instance, the welfare of the birds is paramount but my Bird Garden is also a very satisfying and beautiful place, both to be in and to look out upon.

DESIGN

I wanted the focus of bird activity to be centred on the part of our garden that we can see from the kitchen window, so that Peter and I, and our visiting family and friends, could enjoy a grandstand view. Throughout the year we are able to watch many more birds from within the house than we could outside in the garden, where we often inadvertently disturb them with our activities. We purposefully designed the garden to incorporate many features that would bring an abundance of birds close to the house and into the frame provided by the kitchen window. With the backdrop of an existing native hedge, the stage was already well set when we arrived in 1987. We just needed the right "props" in the foreground, some essential "furniture" and some exciting bird-friendly planting. Naturally, the results would also depend enormously on the wildlife-friendly habitat we could create in the other four areas of the garden; the pond, meadows, woodland, hedgerows, compost heap and artificial habitat-boosters contributing to the overall health of our garden ecosystem.

Some birds visit our Bird Garden regularly and reliably throughout the year and breed close by. Others call in from time to time, varying their habits with the seasons and the availability of food elsewhere. Of this group, some are resident on our land but are timid or rely exclusively on wild food. We also receive summer or winter visitors who may stay for a season or just call in briefly on their travels. There are a few birds, such as owls and swallows that are seen on other areas of our five acres of land but not actually in the Bird Garden.

PATHS, PERGOLAS, FEATURES AND PRACTICAL ACCESS   My vision for this garden began at the point where I needed to blend house with garden. The wide gravel and paving path was to turn at right angles from the Frog to the Bird Garden, to skirt the east side of the house. There were to be generously plant-clad pergolas extending from the house, crossing the gravel surround and casting intermittent shade and interesting shadows. For spring and summer treats, pots with bulbs and tender perennials would be set among the tangle of entwining plants. In winter the same pots could display coloured winter stems and could contain cut stems with seed-heads for the birds. Right through the seasons I would be able to admire the plants and savour the scented and aromatic ones while on my daily feeding-round – one of the highlights of my day.

There would be a concentration of attractive features for the birds, most of them positioned where they could be seen from the house windows. Similar feeding and nesting apparatus would be scattered around other parts of the garden; inviting them exclusively to one spot would make the birds over-conspicuous to predators and overcrowding can result in hygiene problems where feeders are concerned.

Some birds enjoy the challenge of visiting manmade feeders whereas some are less adventurous or simply not designed to feed in that way. Many birds are adapting to our garden environment and learning new tricks (such as hovering), but a few remain unimpressed or not physically equipped for the antics involved in hanging onto the edge of, or upside down from, a natty, manmade feeding device.

My 7m- (8yd-) diameter "floral carpet", as I call it, is designed as a safe and decorative arena to accommodate and show off both ground-feeding birds and those visiting the bird-bath and sand-bath. I wanted this gravelled planting space to be in the middle of the garden but to look part of the whole gently curving pattern rather than like a bed plonked in the centre of the lawn. I sketched the lines of the design of this garden without lifting pencil from paper and this left me with a fluid-looking horseshoe shape, defined by narrow ribbons of surrounding grass. In the high-profile centre, flagstones could be set into a slightly mounded gravel bed, spiralling inward to the large central bird-bath, and diminishing in size as they reach the epicentre. I called the whole feature "the swirl".

PLANTING BRIEF

As with the Frog Garden, I was lucky to have a particularly bountiful stretch of hedgerow bordering the Bird Garden. This natural hedgerow "larder", with the ground below, has most of the provisions needed to sustain many adult birds and their nestlings. With our two mature oaks nearby, it would be difficult to better the planting formula. Some entomologists estimate that between one and two thousand different insects live in such mature, mixed hedges.

Many wildflowers arrive in borders, either by intention or default. As usual, I would be quite prepared to negotiate with the "volunteer arrivals" (the weeds) provided they were the right colour, but common sense would have to prevail if I needed to prevent things getting completely out of hand. A range of native plants would attract the right sort of insects for the birds to feed on and the hedgerow plants would supply fruits, nuts, berries and seeds for the vegetarian residents. There is a drainage ditch and bank which forms an integral part of the hedge. This is a bonus zone of habitat for wildlife as it offers dry, rooty crevices and crannies as well as moist and muddy places for many months of the year.

BORDERS Admittedly, not every single one of the plants I selected for this garden had special bird appeal, but 90 per cent of plants, as well as being beautiful, would also provide food and habitat for birds and/or for interrelated wildlife. I chose plants that would not only help provide a natural diet for birds but would give added protection for them when they were roosting or nesting. My selection included thorny or spiny shrubs and those that form dense thickets, some of which would be evergreen. I picked one or two selected trees to screen the intrusive view of nearby houses and others to help shelter the garden from the prevailing south-westerly winds. I would plant cornus and willow to continue the winter effect of coloured stems which was a feature of the adjoining Frog Garden. I love to watch plants whose vision is enhanced by gentle summer breeze or even wild winter wind. Swaying grasses and fluttery, silver-backed leaves would meet the criteria for making a windswept site a dramatic one.

PINK FLOWERS AND PLUM-COLOURED FOLIAGE For orchestrating a prolonged season of flowering with a wide range of bird-friendly and people-pleasing plants, pink is an good colour to work with because there is a wealth of choice, so I chose pink as the principal colour for the flowering plants, supported by foliage in plum, bronze, burgundy and ruby shades, according to the variations in the pink tints and tones of the flowers. Among my pink selection I wanted to include scented plants such as viburnums, lilies and roses and position them where, in my year-round sequence of daily feeding-rounds, my meetings with them would be intimate. If I wanted to grow a few tender perennials in pots, then this much visited and viewed part of the garden would be the place where they would give me the most pleasure and be guaranteed to receive my full attention.

HOUSE-WALL HABITAT Birds appreciate the warmth and protection which buildings can offer. If lavishly plant-covered, as ours were intended to be, the walls would offer warm roosting sites and space for safe nesting places. The support wires for the climbers were to be held in place about six inches from the wall so there was a spacious gap where birds could benefit from the microclimate that is eventually created. The leaf litter at the base of the wall plants would be an important asset in providing insect cover and winter warmth for birds.

CONSTRUCTION

PATH, PERGOLA AND STEPS We continued the path around the house using the same low-cost materials for the pergola as for the Frog Garden (see page xx). Peter and I wished we could have afforded chunky green oak but had to make do with regulation, treated softwood. The construction was simple and also low-budget, using bog-standard 8 by 8cm (3 by 3 in) uprights and 12 by 4cm (5 by 1.5 in)

cross-members. They looked very ordinary until I dressed them to have a more "organic" appearance. One post is now trimmed around with hemp rope, which the birds like to use for beak wiping after a greasy dinner of home-made bird-pudding (see page 78). Another post is now a pillar of ivy. By annual hard pruning of the new growth of the latter, and training the leading stem in a spiral, I have created a gnarled, woody, evergreen column. It is arguable whether the post supports the ivy or vice versa! Other posts are decorated with spirals of willow or hazel stems.

We adorned our pergola with hand-crafted willow features for birds to feed, perch, roost and nest, and used fragrant plants, such as honeysuckle, lilies and *Rosa* 'Debutante', to cover the walls and the woodwork.

Close to the house, where there was a change of level to deal with, Peter used old railway sleepers to make a set of shallow steps and we gravelled the surface in between. We used these same economy materials to make a path to intersect one of the borders and allow access to the adjacent gardens.

FEATURES AND PLANTING SPACES   The "floral carpet" or "swirl" needed to be well drained, so we employed topsoil from the path excavations to raise the ground level with some gravel mixed in to help. The flat stone slabs that form the spiral design would also provide additional conditions to help certain plants to thrive and they would doubtless be useful for snail-bashing thrushes. At the centre I used a tufa mix (see Frog Garden, page 26) to make a shallow bird-bath that is slightly more generously sized than any I have seen in garden centres. Some birds, such as sparrows, enjoy communal bathing and sometimes small birds will actually stand at the edge and take a shower in the tidal wave caused by larger birds splashing about

in the centre. The swirl and the borders were prepared with our usual diligence; we first ensured that the area was entirely free of grass and perennial weeds before thoroughly conditioning the soil with well-rotted manure. Only then did we begin to plant the first trees and shrubs.

THE BIRD-FRIENDLY LAWN   Although I intended to minimize grass mowing, I make no apologies for mowing the small proportion of the grassland which is central to the design of this garden. The lawn also defines and strengthens the design and is cool and comfortable to walk on. Some birds really do appreciate fairly close-mown grass when foraging for invertebrates, so my green "ribbons" of turf form part of the varied habitat in the Bird Garden. The fact that the turf is, by chance, composed of approximately 50 per cent white clover is a bonus; we have a self-feeding lawn that enriches itself with its own nitrogen, which is naturally manufactured by this leguminous plant's own roots. Our lawn is always verdant and lush, full of worms for the birds and with the bonus of the little white flowers to keep our bees happy.

A pattern of close-mown grass paths surrounds this swirl, bringing the insect- or worm-seeking visitors, such as pied wagtails, robins, blackbirds and thrushes to the fore. Thrushes are a fine spectacle and, though increasingly scarce, a joy to behold. Unfortunately they are easily scared away by the more competitive birds – blackbirds being the main antagonists. Starlings are the masters of organic leather-jacket control, penetrating and aerating the turf with their mighty strong beaks as they search for the grubs. Jackdaws, with their even more powerful beaks, drop in from time to time, cantering sideways endearingly across the lawn as they forage. I am not sure of the criteria that move them to desert their usual feeding territory around our stables, but I think perhaps the older birds become more domesticated.

Although swallows nest in our stables and outbuildings, from the Bird Garden we only hear and see them flying above us and swooping to catch insects on the wing. Buzzards, too, can be heard and seen overhead, but much higher up, soaring over the open hills and woodland that surround us.

Vibrant Japanese blood grass (*Imperata cylindrica* 'Rubra') punctuates the floral carpet of insect nectar plants, including oreganos, thymes and *Geranium striatum*.

We rarely see more than a pair of pied wagtails in this garden at one time. They usually forage on the lawn but just now and again, presumably when insects are short, these most delightful, uncompetitive birds will make their selection from the least complicated and open of our seed-holders. The related grey wagtails are just a hop away in the Frog Garden, where they are drawn to the recently enlarged ponds.

PLANTING

When we began this garden, the first thing we did was to allow the existing eastern boundary hedge to grow tall. Peter cut and laid (and regularly trimmed) a stretch of it to invigorate and thicken the base and to make dense, rich habitat which is ideal for nesting. The remaining hedge is allowed to continue to grow tall and produce hips and berries on the mature wood. There is always a hub of activity as hundreds of birds chatter, perch, forage and make their homes among the branches. The mixed native hedgerow plants provide first-class living accommodation for the birds and are a vital source of food. The oak offers acorns for jays, wood pigeons, great spotted woodpeckers and nuthatches. Hawthorn, blackthorn, bryony, nightshade, elder,

guelder rose and privet provide a sequence of luscious berries. In particular, brambles supply seed and flesh for blackbirds, warblers and finches. Greenfinches are partial to rosehips, while the robins seek out spindle berries. Ivy berries are the last in the season to form and cater for wood pigeons, robins and blackcaps. In spring, willow – especially goat willow – attracts early insects to supply the birds with body-building protein. Among the herbaceous hedgerow species, numerous "weed" seeds also supply part of their nutritious diet. Chickweed, colt's-foot dandelion, groundsel and sow thistle are by no means the gardener's first choice of wildflower, but they are fine in the hedgerow and if they inevitably turn up in borders then at least it is a comfort to realize they do have value. I know that finches like the seed of nettles, but I try to confine my nettles to wilder parts of the garden.

The shape of birds' beaks gives a strong clue as to their required or preferred diet. Some, such as finches, have short, robust beaks that are brilliantly engineered for seed dehusking. Others, such as blackbirds and starlings, have longer, more slender beaks for ferreting out worms, grubs and insects.

GARDEN TREES My first choice of tree is appropriately named for this garden. The bird cherry has black berries on the beautiful bronze/purple leaves of the pink-flowered form (*Prunus padus* 'Colorata'). These berries are devoured early in the season but I must admit I am not convinced the coloured form is as remarkably well-flavoured as the slightly less ornamental, white-flowered parent (*Prunus padus*) which is host to a seemingly bottomless supply of insects while appearing to be quite cosmetically unchallenged by them. This tree is constantly full of birds, particularly tits – blue tits, great tits, coaltits, long-tailed tits and marsh-tits – all of which also visit the bird-feeders. There are also tree-creepers, flycatchers and occasionally nuthatches in the bird cherries. Each day I watch the birds busily working the stems but I can never determine exactly which bugs or insects they find so thrilling.

Crab apples produce masses of fruit which the birds eat once they begin to rot. The purple-foliaged, red-flowered *Malus* 'Red Glow' is always heavily laden with delightful pink fruit. The ornamental cherry, *Prunus cerasifera* 'Nigra', has brownish-

When we cut and laid our boundary hedge we recycled some ash branches to make an "eco seat" to offer a good habitat for wildlife and a place for us to pause to enjoy our plants and the birds they encourage and support.

purple leaves with pale pink flowers, the buds of which are beloved by bullfinches. It doesn't worry me if they pinch them because, when it comes to non-fruiting ornamentals, potential fruit and berry pickers (bird or human) are not deprived as a result of their sabotage. It was not long before the trees became of significant size to be used as song posts and this cherry tree, with its upright form, was one of the first.

BIRD SONG AND ACTIVITIES   Fortunately for us, when birds broadcast their territorial rights to each other it manifests to us as the most delightful song. Blackbirds and robins are the tamest birds and yet among the most aggressive when it comes to fighting for territory. Dunnocks are also charming songbirds but far more timid. Wrens and thrushes bring indescribable joy with their sweet song and are always around the garden, though not in large numbers. These two are very independent as far as supplementary feeding is concerned. Blackcaps, those very fine songsters, whose music is often likened to a nightingale, usually only come to our feeders in winter. Of the other birds in the same (warbler) family, chiffchaffs and garden warblers are summer visitors, the former bringing its distinctive sound to our hedgerows. Peter developed a finely tuned ear for distinguishing individual birdsong and an astute eye for the rare or unusual visitors, such as bramblings and reed buntings, which have pitched up on odd occasions.

Tree-creepers are most furtive in pursuit of their insect prey and stay close to the bark of trees, always ascending them from the bottom to the top of the trunk. I only see these tiny birds in winter but I expect they are around all year. Nuthatches are larger, more striking and conspicuously coloured, and work the tree trunks from top to bottom. We seldom notice spotted flycatchers in the Bird Garden; although they are around, they conduct themselves in a secretive way. We obtain a better view of them in our poly-tunnels where they find easy pickings as unfortunate insects get trapped against the polythene. Goldcrests also flit about among the tree branches and stems. These are the tiniest and one of the most engaging of our British birds. They can be distinguished by their neat little mohican-style gold caps and bold eye stripes.

There are herbaceous plants among the pink and plum-coloured shrubs, including
Berberis 'Harlequin'. The chocolate-scented Cosmos atrosanguineus glows brightly beside
dusky pink Sedum telephium 'Matrona', which has long lasting and attractive seed-heads,
often harbouring tiny insects that attract garden warblers.

SHRUBS I like the continuity provided by using garden forms of native hedgerow plants to integrate garden and boundary. The purple form of our wild elder (*Sambucus nigra* 'Purpurea') has scented and very beautiful pink flowers, bronzy-purple foliage and black berries that are as well received as those of its native cousin. Purple hazel (*Corylus maxima* 'Purpurea') has large purple leaves with nuts to match. Jays are the only birds with strong enough beaks (and the inclination) to extract the kernels. I have never seen them at work but I have found nuts showing evidence of their industry. They leave the shell more fragmented and less neatly accessed than dormice, which also feed on hazel nuts. There is an interesting coloured form of our native blackthorn, *Prunus spinosa*. The soft plum-coloured foliage, which turns red in autumn, looks striking when combined with the blue-black sloe berries. Plants such as this may be a new way forward for the gardener with an interest in wildlife. They offer the glamour of a garden plant with, hopefully, all the specific, associated benefits that the native parentage offers in terms of food and habitat.

Lonicera rupicola var. *syringantha* is a rather rambling shrub that is early-flowering and sweetly scented, and has just a few red berries for birds. This is a tough cookie and uncomplainingly puts up with the occasional violent assault necessary to keep it vaguely in bounds. If allowed to grow reasonably unimpeded, it forms a densely-branched thicket with narrow grey-green leaves. Thickets provide a remarkable level of protection against the cold wind. I'd hate to be without this rather wayward hunk of a plant and so would the gang of sparrows who, for some reason, love to socialize in the maze of stems in winter, reminding me of giggling gangs of little children.

Lonicera pileata and L. *yunnanensis* form dense evergreen cover for winter shelter and well-secreted nesting sites. They make quite a secret of their purple berries too. I have never witnessed the birds eating them but maybe they enjoy them as much as the pink berries of the deciduous *Symphoricarpos chenaultii* 'Hancock', which holds its pink berries at the end of long wands of tightly massed cascading stems. There is one other impenetrable shrub which makes outstanding bird habitat: *Cotoneaster conspicuus* is a strapping, arching, evergreen shrub with powerful visual impact and is also an outstanding provider for wildlife. Honey-bees are drawn in their hundreds to the masses of pink-tinged flowers in spring and, occasionally, there is even an early butterfly or two. Oddly, the berries have no appeal for the birds but it is the tangled network of tough branches that draws several species to compete for shelter and to roost and breed within its confines. Sparrows, dunnocks and blackbirds are almost always scuttling about in its stiff skirts and, if I throw some food nearby, I can be quite certain of one or another popping out from within.

The "pheasant berry", or *Leycestera formosa*, is a sadly underrated shrub in my opinion. I love both its pink and red dangling flowers and the red berries which form while flower buds are still coming out. Where feasible, I allow it to self-seed — which it does with great generosity — because it has both bird and bee appeal, as well as great personality and shiny green stems that add a verdant element to the winter scene. The apple-blossom-pink-flowered *Chaenomeles speciosa* 'Moerloosei' has quince-like fruits which, when they finally begin to rot, offer emergency rations in harsh, late-winter weather.

By autumn, the pink flowers in this garden give way to red hips of dog roses and the berries of *Cotoneaster horizontalis* and C. 'Coral Beauty', which spread along the ground and hug the house walls. In the border there is a very dark maroon-stemmed dogwood (*Cornus alba* 'Kesselringii') which has bronze foliage. The berries are white and soon eaten in September and then, after the yellow autumn leaves are shed, the gleaming bare stems steal the show when set against the varied red, yellow and orange stems of willows and other cornuses. Imagine how stunning our birds look in such a dramatic setting!

Fieldfares and occasional redwings call in and raid the fruit and berries in late autumn and winter. I love to see them but they cause dissent amongst the blackbird population, which seems to resent this daylight robbery of their winter provisions.

SCENTED PLANTS AND OTHER TREATS FOR US Closer at hand, *Lonicera x purpusii* frames the window and is a favourite place for small birds to shelter. During mid to late winter, we relish the astonishing fragrance of this shrub when the bare branches are covered in flowers. The power of the perfume defies belief when you consider the diminutive size of the flowers. It has a few succulent red berries which the blackbirds take gratefully in early spring when most other berries are gone. Other scented plants include *Viburnum farreri* and *V. x burkwoodii* which flower in

sequence from about November to May and they have a few berries to follow. When selecting a healthy, scented, pink-flowered climbing rose, I chose 'Debutante'. She is smothered in clusters of flowers for several weeks, produces a few small hips, and then pops up a few surprise and welcome sprays of flowers right up until Christmas. She spreads sinuous arms right across the east side of the house and I train a few of her long stems along the cross-bars of the pergola. *Lilium* 'Pink Perfection', grown in pots at the base of the pergola, has splendid steely-pink trumpets and a rich and penetrating scent in June; later there are the reflexed, spotted petals of *L. speciosum* var. *rubrum*. They

There are moments of pure human indulgence as I pause from bird-feeding duties to imbibe the extravagant fragrance of the aptly named Lilium 'Pink Perfection', partnered by the perfectly colour-matched *Diascia rigescens*.

both attract hoverflies but I admit I have seen no noticeable direct benefit to birds, unless they eat the seeds.

The chocolate-scented *Cosmos atrosanguineus* is a real indulgence for Peter and me, and any chocoholic garden visitors. Although it has no obvious bird-appeal, it draws plenty of bees to its amazingly rich claret-coloured flowers. All these fragrant plants give me great joy as I wander round on my daily bird-feeding schedule. This part of the garden is not exclusively for birds – there are other creatures to consider and this includes the owners! Gardening "in tune with nature" also requires that our human nature is considered and all our senses satisfied.

As an extra treat for myself I grow a few tender and not-so-tender perennials in pots; *Diascia rigescens* and *Verbena* 'Silver Anne' associate most pleasingly with each other and with the nearby *Penstemon* 'Apple Blossom' and an airy pink gypsophila. With regular dead-heading and an occasional dose of seaweed liquid, the verbena and diascia flower continually for about five months of the year. They sprawl through, and are loosely supported by, some of the woven structures which also function as bird perches. In winter these same woven supports hold arrangements of harvested seed-heads.

THE FLORAL CARPET CENTREPIECE   From the framework of my kitchen window, I painted a living picture – a set staged for the extra dynamics of colour, sound and movement provided by the birds. The spiral of stones in the floral carpet have now become obscured by the tapestry of plants, such as thrift, thyme, marjoram and ajuga, that thrive in this open, sunny, well-drained site. This pretty carpet of flowering plants is punctuated by waving grasses and the vertical accents of dieramas, whose graceful, swaying stems yielding to the slightest breeze are often momentarily bent to the ground by finches raiding insects for their young (or eventually taking their seeds). Bullfinches do a bit of spasmodic blossom- and berry-raiding and visit "the swirl" from time to time. They look particularly striking and add to the effect of the combined colours I have used.

To echo the motion provided by the birds, I use delicate grasses such as the wispy *Stipa tenuissima*, and waving foxtail barley grass, *Hordeum jubatum*, which sparkle with

Poetry in motion! Barley grass (*Hordeum jubatum*) is one of the most admired plants in the garden. Steely-pink flower heads gracefully bow and dance in the breeze.

dew and seem to dance demurely amongst the more static plants. The barley grass is one of my most cherished plants. I often stand transfixed by its beauty and the sheer splendour of the natural "choreography" of the dancing movements of its pink-sheened flowers as they softly twist and sway from side to side. The ornamental grasses seem to interest the birds so I think they must attract insects to their flowers and seed-heads, and to the foliage which forms good insect habitat as the clumps mature. Old stems and leaves are certainly a bonus when it comes to selecting durable nesting materials.

I try to use such plants in a way that concedes to the extraordinary effects of light and shade. For instance, the glowing red blades of the Japanese blood grass (*Imperata cylindrica* 'Rubra') are best placed here in open ground where the sunlight can penetrate all around. In fact, they look to me as if they are illuminated by a force of light drawn through their roots and fuelled by the dynamic force of earth's energy. The emerald green, combined with the dual blood and ruby reds, make the plant versatile in complementing different ends of the pink/plum/red colour spectrum of flowers and other foliage. It is noteworthy how there is a mellow reflection of these colours in the plumage of some of the birds – male chaffinches and bullfinches in particular. Perhaps this takes "set design" to an extreme level, but my kitchen window frames a fabulous living picture and I never tire of watching the scenes unfold.

THE BIRDS Seldom has there been a prettier event than this year when Peter and I stood transfixed as we watched a small group of garden warblers at work picking the aphids off a self-set *Angelica sylvestris* 'Purpurea'. Their antics seemed to give them a need for refreshment and they made sorties to the nearby bird-bath to drink and bathe together. In and around this same bed, dunnocks, sparrows, chaffinches, greenfinches and occasionally yellowhammers forage for the seed I scatter. Collared doves are one of my favourite birds and I love to hear their soft cooing calls and to watch them feeding here. I have a soft spot for their heftier and often quarrelsome relations, the wood pigeons, which regularly drink from the bird-bath and satisfy their hearty appetites. It is a bit unnerving when they haul out long stems of thyme

Sometimes a stunning and useful nectar plant, such as *Angelica gigas*, will have unexpected extra wildlife attributes and discreetly harbour insects that attract birds to feed among its flower- and seed-heads, adding extra dynamics to an already dramatic image.

for nesting material but the plants somehow survive this rather random and brutal pruning. Choosing aromatic foliage is a good way to disguise the presence of chicks and help deflect predators but I wonder if the chicks benefit in other ways from being hatched into a fragrant world?

Sometimes seed from the bird mix germinates and adds an impromptu touch. Not all of these volunteer plants are appropriate here so some are removed but millet looks most handsome and is left to provide an extra food source. We are frequently visited by pheasants which seem to blend with the autumn and winter shapes and colouring as if camouflage had been an intrinsic part of the design.

CLOTHING THE HOUSE WALLS A tangle of roses, clematis and honeysuckle with one or two berry-laden cotoneasters is a good formula for starting to clothe the walls and provide the habitat birds need. I have mentioned my first choice, the great climbing *Rosa* 'Debutante', which occupies a huge space and is regularly used as a roosting and nesting place. Pruning 'Deb' is a task and a half, but also a labour of love as the end result is a wall-covering extending at least 11m (12 yd) across the house, and with long arms reaching along each of the four cross-members of the pergola.

The even more delicate-looking, tiny-leafed, tiny single-flowered *Rosa* 'Nozomi' makes a perfect companion to thread through, and add extra "armour" to, the ubiquitous *Cotoneaster horizontalis* which I grow all around the house at the foot of the walls. The unassuming beauty and fragrance of the shell-pink 'New Dawn' puts this beautiful rose in the "desert island selection" league, as far as I am concerned. The scent has the perfectly balanced blend of sweetness and aroma that I would choose to imbibe when taking my last breath on earth. Ivy arrived uninvited but it has been allowed to grow within a defined space because, among its many virtues, it creates a valuable evergreen roosting and nesting place for wrens, which also feed on the spiders it harbours. The house walls have no loose mortar so the ivy can do little harm and it helps to insulate the building. In late autumn the flowers are rich in nectar for the late butterflies and in mid-winter its black berries are an extra welcome food source when other natural food supplies dwindle.

PINK WILDFLOWERS AND VOLUNTEERS   Wildflower or weed? It depends on whether we judge the volunteers to be guest or gate-crasher. With a little thinning now and again, ragged Robin, lady's smock and fumitory are most welcome pink-flowered natives that have turned up and work happily with my pink colour-scheme. Herb Robert and campion have their place but need to be confined to it and, in this garden, I prefer them not to stray too far from the hedgerows. I stand accused, justifiably, of being too lenient with some of these plants in the recent past. When we began our garden-making, I was a much stricter disciplinarian but I dropped my guard when, increasingly, I began to value the impact and respect the need for allowing in as many native plants as possible. A heather turned up uninvited and unwanted, but its seeds are useful to birds so I put up with it. They also like the seeds of the marjoram which germinates in all sorts of places so, naturally, I weakly give in and leave the plants untrimmed. If I cared less for birds and more for plants, I would take matters in hand and prevent the mass colonization of dynasties of inferior seedlings. Never mind, they are quite easily thinned out where necessary and weeding aromatic plants is first-class therapy – aromatherapy au naturel, so to speak.

Cotoneasters, such as *C. x horizontalis* and *C. x watereri* 'John Waterer' (seen here), provide a sequence of berries as well as joining the throng of plants on the house walls that help to provide habitat for the summer nesting period.

OTHER SEED-HEADS   Although we dead-head some plants to prolong their flowering period, we leave almost all our last crop of seed-heads for wildlife. Birds visit seed-heads not only for the actual seed content but also for the numbers of insects that visit or set up camp in certain plants – such as the dark, dusky-pink Joe pyeweed (*Eupatorium purpureum*), the fluffy pink meadowsweet (*Filipendula rubra* 'Venusta') and the rather sultry *Sedum telephium* 'Matrona'. All these plants, along with the stately varieties of miscanthus, have a forceful visual impact and make a splendid contribution to the performance of the garden. Birds particularly like the seeds of *Geranium pratense* 'Striatum', the scabious-like *Knautia macedonica* and the purple plantains, which are just a hop away from being truly native.

Three of my most admired late-summer plants also leave a legacy of fine seed-heads. *Angelica sylvestris* 'Purpurea' is a tall, stately plant with purple foliage and stems that perfectly partner its beautiful, umbelliferous, pale pink flowers. With *Actaea simplex* 'Brunette' there is a similar, and possibly even more striking, association of

colour and form, the deeper purple foliage colour being concentrated in its weightier palmate leaves. With a fine, upstanding, vanilla-scented flower spike, loved by Red Admiral butterflies, along with unusual seed-heads as a finale, how much more could any plant offer? *Sanguisorba officinalis* (greater burnet) is also an outstanding and very garden-worthy native plant. It stands about 1.5m (4-5ft) tall with branched flower-heads and bears oval, small but vibrant maroon flowers and seed-heads that eventually turn earthy brown.

WINTER WAYS WITH SEED-HEADS   After a long period of flowering, my tender perennials are eventually taken in for the winter, but the empty pots

Teasels are somewhat free-spirited in the places they choose to grow, but I harvest some mature seed-heads to place in pots to attract goldfinches close to the house, where we can watch their feeding activities in winter.

are not left idle. I fill them with coloured willow and cornus stems which look splendid and also help to support the bunches of seed-heads I import from other parts of the garden. I then have an interesting and ornamental winter arrangement to look out on and one that provides hours of entertaining bird-watching. I include eryngiums, sedums, crocosmia and teasels. The teasels are the best "draws" because they can be relied on, eventually, to bring our brightly coloured goldfinches close to the house. It is fun to try out different plants; one year I may try an edible amaryllis, another I might bring in orache (*Atriplex hortensis*) or sunflower heads from the vegetable garden. I can then determine which birds favour which seeds. Lately, my winter-pot scenario has been in some confusion owing to the seasons being so strange. Teasel seeds usually last well into winter but there have been recent problems with extreme warm, wet weather, which causes the seeds to germinate in the seed heads in autumn. This means some of the food supply will not be available when the birds come to rely on it. I have begun to harvest some teasel heads in September and keep them in a dry place until later in the winter. Then, provided they don't go mouldy, I can deal them out as and when it is timely.

HABITAT BOOSTERS

In our Bird Garden there are many artificial habitat boosters to provide extra roosting, perching, feeding and nesting places. Beginning at the house, our east-facing aspect with its high gable-end is ideal for tit nest-boxes – a choice of three being the maximum there is room for. Birds need their own space and seclusion just as we do, so there is no point in overdoing the numbers of nest-boxes in one space. We can generally accommodate two lots of tits in this garden, at least one blackbird on the house wall, a wren in the ivy just around the corner against the north wall and goodness knows what goes on in the well-occupied hedgerow opposite! Birds bravely make their homes here in spite of the fact that I inadvertently disturb them as I patrol the area at least once a day to fill feeders and water-baths, or as I work in the garden. Remarkably tolerant of quiet, non-confrontational human presence, the home-seekers' criteria seem to be protection from predators, prevailing wind and over-heating. (An exposed south wall can be just too hot for baby chicks.)

For some reason, the tiled house roof is attractive to pied wagtails, which is very gratifying, but I can never discover exactly what it is that appeals to them. The chimney is used as a song-perch and some years we are treated to the melodic music of a resident song thrush so, all in all, our building serves the birds well in many ways.

NEST-BOXES There are many designs and varied constructions for nest-boxes. The RSPB, the British Trust for Ornithology (BTO) and various manufacturers are producing an ever-widening, scientifically designed range to meet the growing need for artificial bird habitat. Different birds have different requirements and some are very specific. As far as possible, I prefer to try to create protected habitat where the birds can nest naturally, but a sprinkling of nest-boxes certainly helps to boost the natural sites and can often act as an extra safeguard against predators. The main things to take into account are camouflage and protection; aspect and access; weather-proofing; hygiene; and whether the bird naturally chooses a ledge or a hole.

With tit-boxes, the exact size of the entrance hole is crucial as to which species will take up residence. A 28mm (1in) hole is correct for tits and nuthatches and 32mm (1¼in) for sparrows. Woodpeckers will sometimes widen the entrance of wooden boxes with sinister intentions towards the resident's eggs or chicks. A protective punched-out metal plate helps prevent their intrusion. A custom-made box, constructed of cement and sawdust, is the answer to some of the problems with safety and hygiene, but I have to say that some of them lack style and others are distinctly aesthetically challenged. Nevertheless, "handsome is as handsome does", so we invested in, and tried out a few of these and the birds seem well satisfied. We also make tit nest-boxes by hollowing out chunky logs, which are then attached to walls or trees. This is closer to the conditions the birds would naturally choose but these homemade ones are difficult to clean out and if I fail to be diligent in the necessary "spring- (or rather autumn-) cleaning", I worry about the hygiene factor when the same sites are used year after year.

ROOSTING POCKETS This is one feature that I particularly delight in designing and crafting. I use a combination of willow and grasses to weave roosting pockets in which some birds may also choose to nest. It is apparently common for several small birds to share cosy overnight accommodation, their combined body warmth helping to centrally heat these roosters. There are all sorts of products on offer commercially but I like to be a bit adventurous with the design and sizes. When I heard that up to 50 wrens have been found roosting in one place, I couldn't resist weaving a "three-door terraced property" which I hid in the ivy. In fact, it was some time before it was hidden away in its final position because it looked so fascinating and attractive that I gave it a season as a "nesting-material dispenser". I incorporated it into the pergola decoration and stuffed it with hair, moss and dried grass so the birds could make their selection and I could have the fun of seeing which bird chose which material. I now have several generations of roosters tucked away all over the garden in safe, sheltered sites. I very much doubt if there are two the same among them because when I begin with a few twigs I never know quite how they will turn out. If one roosting pocket saves even one little life on a freezing night, then a few hours' twiddling will have been well worth the sore fingers!

PERCHING PLACES Queuing and competing for a place at the feeders and bird-bath is an extremely important social issue for birds. For every two or three we see feeding, there are probably dozens enviously waiting their turn. They can use up and waste a lot of precious energy struggling with the logistics of, and contention involved in, acquiring food. The pergolas and the well-selected and carefully positioned nearby garden trees, shrubs and hedgerow, allow them all a chance to gather, "socialize" and sort out an order.

On the ivy-clad pillar I echo the spiral stem pattern by weaving a willow or hazel "helter skelter" from top to bottom, doubling the circumference of the pillar. This is one of several places for dozens of birds to perch or queue for the feeders. Blackbirds and chaffinches, lacking the athleticism of the tits, use some of these perching places as a launching platform to attack the fat-filled coconut halves which hang like bells from the pergolas. Other posts are variously decorated by wrapping them with willow and attaching curious willow objects to them. For instance, willow "cobwebs" decorate the pergolas and are often threaded into the designs of other woven features. One pergola post is perforated with holes into which I cram a mixture of fat and nuts for the woodpeckers, nuthatches and any bird with the ingenuity to extract the food. I am hoping a tree-creeper may visit but it is a healthy sign that they seem content with the natural fare in the garden.

We planted a weeping silver pear (*Pyrus salicifolia* 'Pendula') at a comfortable 10m (11yd) from the kitchen window. Dozens of small birds gather among the dense branchwork, chattering away as they watch for the right moment to approach. Our home-crafted willow and hazel woven features are a great additional asset in this respect, providing many extra perching and tarrying places while the hierarchy is debated. These bare, twiggy perches are a bonus in summer too, because many of the bird activities are otherwise hidden from us by the great covering of dense foliage and flower. I watch every detail of the various birds' behaviour and then weave different items to try and cater for their needs.

Each year I discover new ways of trying to help. For instance, dunnocks are notorious ground-feeding birds but I have made a feeder which they find totally acceptable and regularly use, thanks to the exact position of the willow perch at the entrance. The particular, spherical, open, willow-woven feature is placed about 1.2m (4ft) high in the top stems of a mahonia. A hollowed-out coconut food-holder hangs centrally and one of the horizontal woven stems is just a couple of inches from the opening in the coconut. Now I am trying to discover which their favourite seed ingredient is. (I don't think I am quite a "bird anorak" – yet – but I happen to be very fond of dunnocks!) Different species vary significantly in their behaviour, choice of food and agility in acquiring it. I am not sure which of us is most entertained; our entrancing birds or we who bird-watch, enthralled by their antics, as we breakfast and then (very happily) wash-up in front of our kitchen window.

BIRD-BATHS These double as drinking places and ours is used daily by a great variety of birds, although many of them also use the shallow edges of our wildlife pond in the Frog Garden. It is important that fresh water is unfailingly supplied, especially in very dry or icy weather. Our bird-bath is situated in full central view of the kitchen window, so there is no way we could overlook topping it up. As far as possible I try to use rainwater for this. The fluctuating level of water seems to affect which birds use the bath from day to day and I still haven't fathomed out the criteria, but I don't think it is as simple as "deeper water = bigger bird".

Preoccupation with ablutions can result in golden opportunities for predators to take advantage and attack. Cats are a major hazard to the survival of birds and although for this reason we did not replace our elderly cats when they died, it is difficult to deter the neighbourhood cats from visiting. It would not be appropriate for me to capture these intruders and equip them with collars with warning bells but I am often sorely tempted when I spot them on a furtive mission or, worse, carrying away a victim. Our low surrounding planting allows good vision and decreases the risk that these intruders will creep up and catch the birds unaware as they drink or "scrub up". Keeping their feathers clean, free of parasites and well preened is of paramount importance to birds so they can survive cold, wet weather and fly with maximum efficiency. Good insulation, together with speed and dexterity, can make the difference between life and death when push comes to shove in a hostile world where predators often lurk nearby.

DUST-BATH   Bearing the birds' flight performance in mind, I have recently introduced a large stone saucer of mixed fine soil and coarse sand into the same area (and try to remember to put a lid on it in wet weather – easier said than done!) Dust-bathing is another efficient way of removing parasites and "dry-cleaning" feathers. The tray also contains grit because some of the finches swallow grit to help their process of digestion. I expect they will snub my offering because they share dust-holes and grit with my hens in their run but it will be gratifying if we see a positive result. It is interesting how sparrows relish communal dust-bathing. One year I tipped a barrow- load of fine gravel near the swirl with a view to topping up the surface mulch. The little birds made at least a dozen indentations and so joyfully did they engage in their grooming activities that I was compelled to leave the heap unspread.

HANGING BIRD FEEDERS   My woven-willow feeding "cages" help protect ageing birds from predators, such as the sparrowhawk and the neighbours' cats. They are either suspended from the pergolas or from a bracket on the house wall (the feeders, not the cats!). I weave round or ovoid globes or spheres which are about 45cm (18 in) in diameter and inside them I hang either a hollowed-out coconut shell seed-holder or a metal peanut-holder.

The open weave is amply large enough for birds to move in and out of but the gauge is small enough to confound the attempts of cat or sparrowhawk to catch their prey off-guard. They are, unfortunately, not squirrel-proof, but I sometimes weave a decorative extra willow "skin" to encircle the custom-made metal feeding cages, especially where peanuts are involved. Part of the fun is to find a practical way to make the Bird Garden amusing and glamorous for us, as well as extra safe and appealing for birds. I have actually seen sparrowhawks trap birds in the manufactured metal feeders but never in my willow ones. I find it strangely surreal to have birds fly freely in and out of what appears to be a cage. An amusing deception!

CUSTOM-MADE FEEDERS   The RSPB and the BTO offer excellent, specially designed custom-made feeders and there are all sorts of products on sale at garden centres and pet shops. Some of them function better than others and only one or two of them have much visual appeal. Peanut feeders are usually efficient and some are quite stylish. Seed dispensers never have a very "organic" appearance because of the plastic components. They are designed to keep seed dry and therefore free-flowing, but if water gets in – and it sometimes does – the thing blocks up and wet seed starts to germinate or rot. One or two of the fancier devices are the very devil to take to bits, clean out, dry and reassemble. The viability of the "free-flow" facility may lie in choosing exactly the right seed mix which may just happen to be the most expensive. However, when they do work efficiently they are fine and they save having to do a daily top up – as I do. It depends on whether you are in a position to commit to a regular agenda and whether you regard the exercise as a tedious chore or one of life's pleasures. The most important thing is to somehow provide a regular supply, especially when the weather is harsh or when there are nestlings to rear. Some birds come to depend on us completely to ensure a constant food source and the worst thing would be to let them down and affect their survival. In very wet weather, peanuts can go mouldy before they are eaten and these must be removed to avoid poisoning the birds.

HOMEMADE COCONUT FEEDERS   Coconut shells make good holders for both fat and seed. They can be halved, drilled with holes near the edge, and low down for drainage, threaded with cord or wire and suspended as open-cup or bell-shaped containers. Two or three birds can feed from these at one time, although competition may result in lively confrontation. The open-cup containers are fine in dry weather but when it is wet the seed gets soggy and the birds reject it. As a drier alternative, we carve out an opening into a whole shell and the birds can take it in turns to help

Reading across, from top left: Bluetits approve the concrete nesting box; a young robin perches on a garden seat; a bluetit pauses before entering the coconut feeder; willow-woven features for feeding, perching and roosting; a robin claims his turn on the feeding log; a lonesome yellowhammer joins ground-feeding birds on the lawn; the bird-bath is a good size for the greater spotted woodpecker; woodpeckers explore one of our range of woven feeding devices.

themselves to the dry seed. Some of the birds squat inside, guarding their pitch and feeding voraciously until they are so full I wonder they can fly! They often chuck out the unfavoured seeds, which become a bonus for the ground-feeding birds such as dunnocks and collared doves, and also our garden-orientated pheasants. At night the field mice sometimes move in to the coconut holders and finish off the leftovers. It is quite strange to go to fill the coconut and, on occasions, find it still full of indignant mouse! I have also known geriatric birds use them for night-time shelter.

It is amusing – but time-consuming and certainly inessential – to draw quirky faces onto the face of the coconut and carve these out. I combine the uses of an electric drill and a hack-saw to get the detail required to give them impish expressions. I get quite attached to my little "coco characters" as they become weather-beaten over the years of service. They start off bearded or top-knotted and end up slap-headed and walnut-like. Damaged or "retired" coconuts, having served our resident wildlife well, are eventually secreted securely into the hedgerows as potential roosting or nest sites.

Some of the halved coconuts are suspended as bell-type fat-holders. During cold weather I melt lard, dripping or any left-over fat, stir in some flour, cereals and small seeds and pour the mixture into the shell as it begins to re-set. An hour or so in the fridge and the "bird pudding" is firmly set and ready to hang up. Birds such as blackbirds, robins, chaffinches and starlings manage to alternate hovering and "missile" attacks to snatch the odd bite from the lower edges. I must admit I worry a little about this. Do they use up as much (or more) energy in acquiring the food as they gain from consuming it? Hovering is said to use up massive energy reserves and propelling oneself off the ground to make an upward spear-attack must similarly clock up a fair few kilowatts. I suppose it is wrong to doubt the birds' judgement in energy expenditure. Most creatures are more astute at measuring resources than mankind seems to be!

Some birds are well designed to hang upside down and can cling to such receptacles without any effort or needing to weigh up the logistics. The tits, for example, have the advantage over the others in that they can thereby feed very easily and reach any fat in the deepest recesses of the bell. Bearing this in mind, I can shape the bells and/or adjust the food levels accordingly. When natural food supplies are more abundant, or if I want to single out the smaller tits for special treatment, I cut the rations and just smear a daily portion of the fat mixture right inside the bell. It helps if the inner surface of the coconut is roughened up so that the fat sticks more firmly. The only downside to preparing coconut-shell features is sorting out the actual coconut flesh. My birds will eat a limited amount but mould attacks the white kernel before they can consume it all. Mouldy food is as bad for birds as it is for us so I gouge out the flesh to make a clean, long-lasting receptacle. I then feed them the chunks of coconut, which I wedge into some of my willow woven items. At nesting time it is better to grate the coconut to avoid any chance of chicks choking on oversized offerings. The long-tailed tits are particularly attracted to this food so I freeze some of the coconut flesh to have in reserve to supply regular rations over the winter. I have several of these feeders so that I have spare ones to interchange while soiled ones are cleaned out. Hygiene is an important part of any animal husbandry – birds included. I use boiling water and sometimes bicarbonate of soda as a safe cleaner but there are also special disinfectants (and brushes) now on the market to help with bird-feeder hygiene.

LOG FEEDERS A very simple fat-feeding device can be made by drilling holes in a log, sticking a hook in the top and suspending it. The holes are then stuffed with food, such as a fat, cereal and seed mix. It is possible to buy these ready-made but we prefer to choose a large, chunky, interesting-shaped branch, "plant" it in the ground and go to town with the drill, making holes of varied diameters. We may use a branch of hazel if pruning or coppicing has been necessary but sometimes we chat up the electricity board tree surgeons and get cast-offs when they clear the local power-lines. The wider the drilled hole, the easier it is to push the fat in; the deeper the hole, the more chance of leaving a deep reserve for the spotted woodpeckers, which can probe further with their long beaks. Sometimes they deepen or expand the holes to their own design! Smaller holes are left unfilled for insects to shelter or breed in, and all the holes are horizontal to prevent water gathering inside.

When the branch eventually begins to look tatty, we retire it into the hedgerows or hedge bottom to become exclusively insect habitat. As it biodegrades it continues to feed and house a changing range of insects and also fungi. We can start again with a new branch each year. This exercise keeps us entertained and the product is a great habitat provider – a winner all round.

APPLE BASKET We store several trays of apples for the winter, sharing the harvest with the birds as, one by one, the fruits inevitably begin to rot. I became rather tired of treading squelchy, rotting fruit into the gravel where the blackbirds had chased them offside. I tried skewering them onto a hazel stick, like an apple kebab, but they soon ended up underfoot again. Eventually I came up with a solution; yet another sphere but this one made with twisted willow (*Salix babylonica* var. *pekinensis* 'Tortuosa') which makes a fascinating object of curiosity. First I weave a globe with a dense skin of intertwined, shiny, wiggly stems. I then pull it apart and, using extra willow stems, reinforce two or three entrance holes for the birds' access and for me to drop in a daily ration of apples. This neatly contains both the fruit and the birds, which can feast away in safety, seclusion and a degree or so of shelter.

The apple basket is held on a tripod of stout hazel stems and placed near the house where blackbirds often lurk, especially in cold weather. Of course, some other apples are chucked further away onto the lawn to provide for birds which do not care to visit the feeders or make a public exhibition of themselves. There may be good sense in birds choosing the natural approach because rotting apples attract the worms and other invertebrates that inhabit the lawn. Thrushes, for instance, prefer a carnivorous diet and eat fruit only as a last resort. A wormy apple would be a bonus for them.

BIRD-TABLE   Peter made our bird-table, roughly following the design of an original, custom-built RSPB one, but giving ours a distinctly rustic character of its own. The roof is "thatched" with strips of split hazel stems and it is set onto the branched top of a mature piece of hazel wood, gleaned from our winter coppicing programme. The table is set within the protective skirts of the prickly *Berberis thunbergii* f. *atropurpurea* 'Harlequin', making it pretty well cat-proof or at least slowing the rate of feline harassment and giving birds time to forestall an attack. The original construction incorporated a nest-box but this is said to be confusing and disruptive for brooding birds, which need seclusion and are very territorial. However, our original apparatus had always had particular appeal for great tits, which took up residence and successfully reared large broods for several years in succession. For their sakes we repeated the design in spite of the somewhat contentious planning regulations – but decided to compromise. We use the bird-table as a feeding-station only occasionally during the worst mid-winter weather, leaving it free as a regularly used maternity unit in the breeding season. I should point out that if this bird-table happened to be the only feeding-station in the garden, I would not allow the dual-purpose facilities and I would make a firm choice between feeding or nesting.

FEEDING "PLATTERS" One of the great joys of sharing a garden with multitudes of birds is to watch them at close quarters. My pergolas bring them within a few yards of the window, and the wall-planting which frames the windows brings them within inches. Arguably, the close proximity to windows may invite disaster with birds crashing against the glass but I believe there may be a case for inviting them close enough to familiarize themselves with the vagaries of glass and thereby teach them to avoid catastrophe. Who knows? Anyway, to bring them into close perspective, I weave an intriguing object resembling a primitive tennis racket or a carpet beater, the "handle" of which I persuade into the branch-work of the wall shrubs surrounding the windows and secure it with string. I then have a platform (or platter, as we call it) in which to incorporate a coconut feeder-cup for seed, and for crumbs which I can conveniently add through the open window. This amounts to a rustic extension to the window sill – which has just set me thinking ...

DISTRIBUTION OF FEEDERS Perhaps this is the moment to point out that it is possible to overdo the feeding-stations in one area. I use some of my feeders in rotation, catering for the slightly varying appetites during the year. To overfeed is wasteful and a surplus can attract unwanted visitors, such as rats. The other problem is that a heavy concentration of birds in one place will inevitably attract predators such as sparrow hawks. Overcrowding may also create hygiene problems and increase the risk of infectious diseases spreading among the birds. To avoid these potential problems, I distribute some of the daily food quota in other parts of the garden and on the other sides of the house, and rotate the use of some of the feeding- stations, resting one or two at a time and scrubbing any soiled apparatus. I crank up the amount of food in adverse weather conditions, or when the adults are struggling to meet the appetites of a hungry brood. My birds leave me in no doubt whatsoever when they are in need. In fact some of the ailing and geriatric birds seem to throw themselves on our mercy and, in their "twilight days", come right up to me each day for special titbits.

VISITING BIRDS Finches are a regular part of our bird community as are house sparrows, which live and work in little flocks that, I am happy to say, are increasing in numbers each year. They have become increasingly ingenious in adapting to using feeders. Chaffinches (like robins) have also learned new skills in hovering in order to extract fat from our coconut "bells". They prefer to feed on the ground but I think they are increasingly adjusting their habits. Certainly our feeding "platters" are very much to their liking. Greenfinches are almost always in this garden, often arguing with each other and taking advantage of the food we provide but becoming conspicuous by their absence when they go off on feeding forays for a short while in autumn. Bullfinches have quite recently begun to use the feeders in mid-winter but more often we see them taking seed from plants such as oregano, which self-seeds in abundance. The spectacular goldfinches much prefer to frequent our meadows and more open surrounding hedgerows. However, they cannot resist my winter display of teasels and will take peanuts and wild bird-seed mix when their natural food sources are scant. The canary-like siskins usually appear at the feeders for a while in cold weather although, since our alders have matured to provide their most favoured seeds, we see them less often in the Bird Garden. Similar-looking but ground-feeding by nature, yellowhammers also venture in from the hedgerows when the going gets tough in winter. Blackcaps (Peter's favourite songbird) seem to find an abundance of food in our trees and hedgerows but come to the feeders from time to time, especially in winter, giving us a rare chance to see them at close quarters.

The tit family are well represented and particularly welcome our supplementary feeding in winter and when rearing broods. Great tits, blue tits and coal tits are always around, chattering and chirping to make sure I never miss a beat with handing out their provisions on time. Long-tailed tits arrive in little family gangs from time to time. We usually hear their conversational twittering just before we spot these pretty little "flying mice" which often arrive just before dusk. The very smart marsh tits feed routinely with us in winter and also have a distinctive, high-pitched call. They can easily be confused with coal tits but on close inspection are sleeker and have less white on their heads.

Our one or two visiting nuthatches have no routine that I can fathom but when one does arrive it dominates the peanuts until well re-fuelled. What a stunningly smart bird it is! Greater spotted woodpeckers are also spectacular and exotic-looking. They, too, seem a bit erratic with their feeding patterns but they check in far more often than the nuthatches. When they do feed, provided they are not disturbed, it is as if they are eating for England. We hear the green woodpecker's yaffle more often than we see them. They live close by but only occasionally do they call in to raid an ants' nest or drink from the pond.

SUPPLEMENTARY BIRD FOODS

All the above offerings are to boost the food which occurs naturally in the garden. Contrary to the way it may appear, I do not need to feed vast amounts of these extras because the birds forage on the fruit, berries and seeds plus insects and other invertebrates. It is noticeable how concentrations of birds flock to even tiny plots of organically managed land but, as there is a diminishing amount of chemical-free land to satisfy their needs, popular haunts, such as Sticky Wicket, soon become heavily stocked. This is most gratifying for us but a little supplementary food seems to be required if the needs of the increased population are to be served. Birds can be fed scraps or more conveniently – and consistently – fed with bird seed and nuts, which are readily available in shops or by mail order.

READYMADE FOODS There are one or two points to be aware of when buying or preparing bird food. There are lethal moulds which can affect the peanuts we eat ourselves or feed to birds. Peanuts are a nutritious addition to their diet but they may be affected by aflatoxin, a toxic fungus that can poison birds (and humans). It is vital to purchase seed that has been tested and certified free of disease and sold as "safe peanuts". I order premium nuts from the RSPB or the BTO or from very reliable suppliers, such as Ernest Charles. I am assured by both bird conservation organizations that it is safe – and indeed advantageous – to feed certified peanuts all year, providing the birds cannot take the kernels away whole and risk the possibility of choking their chicks with oversize pieces.

I wonder, therefore, why some less reliable suppliers sell mixed seed with whole peanuts in? The responsible bird-seed companies do not include these nuts in their all-season mixes unless they are finely chopped. There are plenty of mixtures to choose from and those with a high percentage of black sunflower seeds will be most valued. With the black, as opposed to white or striped, seed, it is said to be easier for the birds to extract kernel from husk. Cheap seed mixes often have disproportionate quantities of fillers such as wheat and linseed. I find linseed is fairly universally disregarded by the birds but perhaps that is because I don't have linnets in the garden. Linnets are said to like linseed so perhaps there is an arguable "chicken and egg" case for having a tiny proportion in the mix – just in case they arrive and decide the Sticky Wicket habitat has become favourable. Rape seed seems to find its way into many mixtures. The birds eat it but inevitably seeds are rejected or dropped and often germinate, grow to maturity and flower. Now, can anyone convince me that bird seed merchants can put hand on heart and declare the rape to be GM-free? Cross-fertilization between GM and non-GM rape is inevitable and will be guaranteed to result in some genetic pollution of non-GM rape and certain brassicas. I do wish more gardeners and bird-lovers would press for "reassurance", if only to generate some response from suppliers and from government, and so force the issues of extensive and responsible research, together with much tighter controls.

LIVE FOOD It is possible to buy mealworms and other grubs to satisfy birds with an appetite for meat. Most seed-feeding birds forsake their vegetarian diet when rearing chicks. Baby birds need lots of protein and demands on their parents are immense. I have given my birds these treats on occasions but I prefer to concentrate on creating suitable habitat and managing the garden to encourage a natural and varied food source. This is just one good reason why the wildlife gardener needs to have a generous tolerance of insects and never ever use pesticides. The natural predators, including birds, will gradually sort out a healthy balance.

BIRD PUDDING AND SCRAPS About once a week I melt a block of fat, stir in a mixture of cereals which might include some oatmeal, ground semolina, flour, flaked millet and other seeds. Just lard and brown flour will do and is cheapest. Each day I put the required ration into the coconut fat holders so that it never hangs about getting stale. Of course it would be much easier to buy blocks of prepared "bird cake" but I prefer to do it the hard way so I know what I'm feeding.

Birds' appetites vary but most left-over offerings are gladly accepted. However, I have found feeding of mixed kitchen scraps often attracts crows and starlings whose presence in large numbers can be a bit overwhelming for the small birds normally frequenting the feeders. There are also the questions of keeping the bird-table clean and hygienic, and avoiding cooked foods which might attract rats. I generally stick to seed, nuts, fruit and a little coconut. In very cold spells I make exceptions but I make sure any uneaten cooked scraps are removed at night. Wrens, so minute they can freeze to death in cold spells, are said to accept grated cheese so I sometimes put a little emergency ration in their favourite haunts although there is no certainty they find it before other birds, mice or even our dogs do!

IN CONCLUSION

Our Bird Garden is, of course, only a small part of our five acres of land and naturally the way we plant and manage the rest of our land has a direct bearing on the results. Our other gardens with their special habitat features all help to support birds and – most essentially – the creatures on which they depend. At night we hear the plaintive calls of owls close-by. A few pheasants stray away from local shooting estates and feed with us during the winter – they are all welcome. Our hospitality wavers when starlings bring a rabble of noisy, greedy mates to the feeders and chase off our small birds. It is a shame because, in small doses, they are handsome, amusing characters and their plumage is most striking (as are their evening pre-roosting displays). I admit to a distinct feeling of hostility towards the sparrowhawks, crows and magpies when they attack our smaller birds. However, predators are part of nature's system so the best we can do is to try to create super-safe nesting sites to give our garden birds a fighting chance of survival.

As I close my chapter on the Bird Garden and look out of my kitchen window where all my thoughts began, I feel quite dizzy. It is like a cross between a menagerie and a circus out there with countless birds in the vicinity and dozens of them whizzing around between the plants and all the features we have dreamt up and constructed. As birds forage for food and dispute territorial rights, there is the sound of the combined fluttering of many tiny wings, a chorus of chattering, trilling and twittering interspersed with the odd alarm call and some sweet winter song in the background. Some of these birds have distinctive characters, markings or even unfortunate disfigurements which help us to identify them individually.

The more Peter and I watch our birds, the more we learn. And the more we learn the more we marvel at their beauty and the way they live their lives. I often ponder – do our birds now give us more pleasure than the plants in the garden? The answer is simple: the two interests are inseparable and generate equal joy for all.

THE ROUND GARDEN

This summer nectar-garden attracts thousands of insects, including bees, butterflies and moths, which are hugely beneficial to the garden ecosystem as well as providing food for other creatures.

Contrasting forms and gentle colours mark this close community of cultivated plants, wildflowers and grasses.

THE SAME SAD TALE of lost habitat, together with intensification of farming and countryside management, has affected the range and numbers of insects remaining in Britain. For instance, the survival of certain breeding colonies of butterflies is inextricably linked to the way downland and lowland pasture is grazed, and to the management of traditional hay meadows and woodlands. Mercifully, some of the modern agricultural crops seem to suit some species of bees – just as well for farmers because the bees are vital for the pollination of some major crops, such as oil-seed rape. All the same, some bee species have suffered as a result of foreign, imported broad-leaved plant species introduced into grassland. All these, plus many other contributory factors, have resulted in the fact that a quarter of our 254 bee species are now on the official list of endangered species. Five of our native butterfly species are now extinct and many are in serious decline and need all the help we gardeners can give them.

Huge numbers of useful insects are taken out of the food chain by chemicals purposely designed to eliminate so-called pests. Sometimes, however, it is the secondary, and unfortunate, effect of the chemicals that results in non-targeted species also being wiped out. The importance of creatures at the bottom of the food chain – the thousands of tiny insects and invertebrates we hardly notice – should never be underestimated. Many of these live below the soil surface and are vital to its health as well as that of other creatures – be it insect, amphibian, reptile or mammal – which prey on them, or with whom they may have a symbiotic association.

The subject of genetically modified crops rumbles on and I fear the present halt to procedures is only a temporary amnesty while the public are left to become complacent about the many political, social and environmental issues that need to be debated and resolved. Noone can predict the outcome of the growing of GM crops but some reports have suggested that the crops themselves (and the fact that chemicals are a mandatory part of crop production) could pose an additional hazard to wildlife. If insect-resistant GM crops are let loose in our environment, there will undoubtedly be a knock-on effect on the numbers of garden pest predators, such as ladybirds and lacewings, which may feed on the newly poisoned, yet still surviving aphids that the crop is designed to wipe out. Another real danger is the greater, more "efficient", destruction of weeds as a result of using herbicide-tolerant crops. Weeds are the natural diet for many creatures and for foraging herbivores and nectar-seeking insects this would be a disaster.

For mankind the bottom line is this: we need insects to pollinate many of our food crops, orchards, meadows, gardens, woods and hedgerows, and the implications are pretty grave if they are imperilled. Happily, it is the easiest thing in the world for gardeners to give a helping hand to boost the populations of many of these tiny miracle-makers. Without our network of wildlife-friendly gardens there would be considerably less chance of protecting Britain's diminishing numbers of insects. Butterflies, moths, bees, hoverflies, beetles and other insects are not only fascinating to watch, but join forces to turn vital cogs in the whole incredible ecological system. This is a system that we simply cannot allow to fragment if man and both his indigenous and imported flora and fauna are to co-exist on earth.

GARDEN CONSERVATION   There are many species that can benefit from our "manufactured" habitat, although there will always be those whose requirements remain too specific for the habitats our gardens can provide. For example, if we happen to garden immediately next to a large wood or conservation site, such as a site of special scientific interest (SSSI), we might seduce some of the rarer inhabitants to drop in to feed, but generally it is only about one third of the local butterfly species that one might expect to record in a garden. This may amount to about fifteen butterfly species, but moth species are likely to be much higher – perhaps several hundred!

With the current garden design epidemic of decking, concrete, glass and stainless steel, let alone exotics like banana trees, changing the face of the urban landscape, we must be thankful there are still many of us who want to retain the charm and old-world romance of the traditional "English" garden that wildlife so much enjoys. For a start, there are masses of beautiful wildflowers and fabulous garden plants laden with pollen and positively oozing nectar. It is the easiest thing in the world to choose and grow a few of the best plants. This will massively increase the insect food supply, with the reward of seeing a garden filled with the beauty and vitality of some of the most beautiful creatures in Britain.

THE WILDLIFE BRIEF   I decided to concentrate my collection of insect-friendly plants in a circular garden where I could take a close look at what was going on in the magical world of garden wildlife, and with bees and butterflies in particular. I needed to give prime consideration to the needs of butterflies because they are delicate creatures which appreciate a warm, sheltered place to feed, roost, mate and breed. I understand that, in their natural environment, woodland edges, sunny glades and wide, open rides suit most of them admirably. Although some may cling to the shade more than others, there are many that venture out into open grassland.

I designed the Round Garden by mimicking these "sunny glade" conditions and felt reasonably confident that my formula would also suit the other slightly less habitat-specific insects that I particularly wanted to invite to my insect commune. I tried to cater for the useful pollinating and pest-predating workforce that an aspiring organic grower particularly needs on their side when trying to tip the balance favourably between the creatures regarded as friend and those as foe in the garden.

THE DESIGN BRIEF

I chose a circular design for several reasons: firstly, the concentric circles of paths would enable us to stroll among the plants and closely observe them and their inter-relationship with the visiting insects at work on the feast laid before them. The geometric design had to be considered carefully as I wanted the dissecting paths to cause minimum disturbance to the overall rhythm of the planting. In fact, I foresaw the strong pattern becoming increasingly incidental to the overall blend of colours and the general haze of planting that I hoped would blend together in a painterly way.

Apart from it being an insect sanctuary, I wanted this garden to be extraordinary in a personal way. Circles are said to represent protection, safety and harmony so I assumed that as true for humans and wildlife alike, and made that my starting point. I placed a seasonally changing feature at the epicentre, to be encircled by mounded camomile rings – just hinting at an echo of an ancient henge, labyrinth or maze but without the physical or psychological complications.

This pastiche of fanciful notions formed my mental concept for this garden and I loosely incorporated them into the design. I wanted to encompass my interest in the magic and mystery of circles but without getting too spooked by invoking strange powers I might not understand. I was also drawn to the contemplative aspect of monastic gardens, although I have to admit that my garden feels as if it may have rather pagan overtones! I had an intuitive desire to create a special circular space rather than try to incorporate any informed association with religion, astronomy or meddling with the occult. Be that as it may, there are times when I can distinctly feel strange (but generally comforting) forces and energies.

THE CAMOMILE ENERGY CENTRE   There is no place in the garden to compare with the energy that exists in the centre where a luxurious carpet of aromatic camomile and thyme flourishes, fringed with wisps of airy, silvery-pink cloud grass. These same plants also carpet the two low, encircling, mounded rings which are broken in two places, rather like a small remnant of a maze or labyrinth. But my feature is not intended to confound, confuse, pay penance or have any particular allegorical associations. It is there to complete the calming process that begins when I progress round the paths in an anti-clockwise direction. Anti-clockwise feels good – it "unwinds" me. A mandala is a circular, spiritual space symbolizing the world and the universe. Maybe this was at the back of my mind when I began but I cannot claim the notion was at the forefront. However, within this central space I can feel the drawing force of earth's energies and at the same time imagine a prayer spiralling upwards to heaven. On a more mundane level, and weather depending, this is also an excellent spot for an afternoon nap with my whippets or a glass of whisky of an evening!

From this awesome place I have celebrated 17 Christmases and birthdays and 34 summer and winter solstices; the birth of my god-children; the new millennium; mourned the loss of several loved ones; witnessed the eclipse of the sun and the moon, and seen the Northern lights.

THE VARIABLE EPICENTRE   At the very epicentre of the inner camomile circle I can vary the central feature according to the seasons and occasionally for a special event, such as a gathering of friends for an evening shindig. In this case we might place a mobile wood-burner to warm ourselves and cook by as well as celebrate the element of fire. In spring and autumn I like to reveal the water that lies beneath the earth's surface so there is a tiny, shallow, central well which is usually brimming at these times. In summer the well is dry so I put a lid over it in the form of a sundial and honour the power of the sun. In deepest winter I weave a willow globe as a decorative centrepiece which looks most spectacular when frosted or iced with snow. It embodies a ball of cold, clean air. Thus all the elements of earth, air, fire and water are represented.

THE RINGS OF BORDERS   I wanted to create a space which, rippling outwards, would engulf me in flowering plants and grasses and make me feel as if I was strolling through the borders rather than gazing at them, as is more usual in gardens. In fact, I wanted a sort of stylized, meadow-like plant community that just happened to have an intersecting geometric pattern of paths (rather like a crop circle) and so I made two concentric circles of paths with three straight ones dissecting the beds into segments. The main axial path runs almost due north-south from the French windows of the main room in the house. I tapered the path to create a false perspective to make it look longer than it is.

This garden is a place where we can wander between the beds in quiet contemplation, touching, smelling and closely examining our sensational assembly of plants. I can study and wonder at their interrelationships, both colourwise and with the visiting insects we see at work among the flowers. I deliberately used crisp gravel for the paths that were visible from the main vantage point (the house and forecourt) but in other places I used bark as a softer (and much quieter) option for a path covering.

CURTAIN OR FRAME   It struck me that what I was about to create could be compared with either a large stage set or a huge painting, depending on whether one stood within it or stood back to view it. Whichever way I scrutinized the setting, to complete the analogy I required either ample curtains or a substantial frame to match the proportions and to shelter, contain and embrace, both visually and ecologically. The success of a flower garden of insect food plants would be very considerably boosted by the close proximity of the enclosing, semi-natural habitats that I would use as a surround.

THE ENFOLDING HEDGES AND TREES   To shelter the site I needed a 2m (6ft) rugosa hedge which would yield a wealth of pollen, nectar and hips while forming a tough, shielding barrier since both the plants and the butterflies would need protection in order to thrive. Three metres (ten yards) behind, and parallel with this, a wide hawthorn hedge would clearly define the northern arc of the circle and diffuse the prevailing south-westerly winds while offering excellent wildlife habitat. A little holly and ivy would augment its dual function and add to its appearance. The hedge height needed to be 2.2 m (7ft) at the tallest place in the middle and to taper to 1.3m (4ft), accentuating the circularity of the layout of the garden (the shelter distance is reckoned to be about four times the height of the hedge). My round garden was to be 35m (40yd) in diameter so my hedge would be an effective barrier against the winds that gust down into our valley.

To the south-west, the group of birches which form my nearby woodland garden would provide an additional wind-break. In just the same way, a dozen or so sheltering fruit trees around the perimeter of the garden would help shield and enfold the inner sanctuary. These trees (plums and damsons, and dessert, cooking and crab apples) would be pollinated by bees drawn to the Round Garden in spring and this would ensure a reliable crop of fruit each year.

HEDGEROWS Existing stretches of mature, boundary hedges to the east and west would complete the enclosure and greatly boost the supporting habitat there. As I have stressed, these British native hedgerows are immensely important to all the visiting and resident wildlife. There could be no finer foundation than our benevolent oak, with its accompanying ivy and underplanting of holly. For butterflies alone, the oak is the singular home for Purple Hairstreaks which live high up, feeding on aphid honeydew and laying eggs on the oak tips. There are also many moths among the 300 or so native insects that the oak can host. Migrant birds time their return to feed their nestlings with these caterpillars. The Holly Blue butterfly breeds on holly in the spring, laying her eggs just under the flowers, but is forced to use ivy for her August brood. Ivy comes up with the goods, pollen-wise and nectar-wise, late in the season when there is a diminishing food supply for lingering bees and late-season butterflies such as Peacocks, Red Admirals and Small Tortoiseshells. Brimstones hibernate in thickets of holly and ivy, cleverly disguised amongst the yellowing dead leaves. Christmas must be a generally fearful time for them, when hedgerows are raided for decoration, but not here at Sticky Wicket where such plants are sacrosanct for wildlife, regardless of celebration.

THE UBIQUITOUS NETTLE PATCH As a giant feeding-station, the nectar garden would serve the wildlife well but, when it comes to perpetuating their species, most insects, especially butterflies, need wild plants on which to lay eggs and provide food for their larvae when they emerge to search to satisfy their voracious appetites. Some insects are very specific in these requirements and will only use as few as one or, perhaps, two particular host plants. The plant that is singled out by the highest number of butterflies is, of course, the nettle. We all know how easy it is to grow nettles but for Red Admirals, Tortoiseshells and Peacocks to lay eggs, the plants must be in a sunny, sheltered site. Commas will accept the sort of partially shaded hedgerow site which many of us would be more willing to sacrifice than a prime, sunny spot held sacrosanct for our garden plants. It is hard luck that the full force of the feel-good factor of abandoning unusable or uncontrolled, over-shaded corners to wildlife doesn't always quite hit the spot! Never mind, there are always those early-hatching aphids, which are such well-timed fodder for the first hatching of ladybirds. These aphids will breed on nettles that colonize in the backwoods we are more readily prepared to consign to wildlife.

NEARBY GRASSLAND Many of our British butterflies live and breed in the sort of unimproved grassland that is increasingly eroded from the countryside. Flower-rich meadows are extremely rare, with 98 per cent having been destroyed. When we began to make the Round Garden we had already begun work on several grassland projects and hoped the Meadow Brown butterflies, Gatekeepers, and Common Blues we were beginning to attract would be drawn to the Round Garden if they needed extra sustenance.

The word "meadow" can conjure an image of almost infinite acres of grasses and wildflowers but this does not necessarily have to be so. I have meadows ranging from one acre to just 3m (10ft) square and every one of my grassland projects is uniquely valuable to the variety of creatures for which they provide a home. On the immediate fringes of the Round Garden, there are two small samples of the sort of semi-natural grassland habitats I have created on our land. Neither patch is more than 5sq m (5½sq yd) but I believe that an area even this size would certainly support a few breeding butterflies and moths, and countless other insects.

PLANTING BRIEF

Within this bountiful framework of woodland, hedgerow and grassland, the Round Garden was intended to be rich in herbs and other nectar plants, mixed with and softened among many varieties of ornamental grasses in a relaxed and naturalistic way. From within a sheltered, plant-festooned, willow-woven arbour at the top of the garden, we would sit peacefully and enjoy watching the wildlife, absorbing the gentle progression of colours and imbibing the cocktail of sweet and spicy herbal fragrances that would waft gently towards us from the scented and aromatic plants.

From the house and forecourt, the picture I wanted to paint was inspired by my having often viewed the original plot through a pane of rain-streaked glass in my kitchen window. The late-19th century neo-impressionists, such as Seurat and Pissarro, used dots of colour (pointillism) to create their impressionistic images; I decided I would use a similar, but more linear technique with mine. I would utilize many fine and upwardly aspiring plants and grasses to give me a trickle of vertical brush strokes mirroring the trickles of water that originally captured my imagination.

The impression I looked for differed again when viewing the garden from the camomile at the core of the design. From this standpoint it would feel more like being at the centre of a stage than viewing a picture. As far as possible, I hoped to make the kaleidoscope of gently blended colours link together, like those that appear as a slowly spinning top loses momentum and comes to rest. There would be yet another different perspective when walking round the garden and as each image becomes a backdrop for another. I decided the planting needed to be staged so as to be viewed in progression as I moved in the anti-clockwise direction I instinctively tended to take.

TIMING THE "FLORAL DANCE"   There is a range of early-flowering nectar plants in the other gardens but, to meet the prime-time needs of the insects, the flowering event in the Round Garden would begin in May, peak in August and carry on until the end of October, when the season of insect activity wanes. I needed to keep the planting florally primed during the period when the greatest numbers of insects are creeping, scuttling or flying about. From mid-June onwards the volume of plant growth would swell and the complete floral picture would begin to form as the insect population built.

SELECTING TRULY UNMODIFIED PLANTS   Where there is a choice, single forms of garden plants are far more useful to wildlife. I can't think of an exception, but there is bound to be at least one which will be stoutly defended by some knowledgeable and observant plantsman. Single flowers display their stamens prominently and very often the petals have conspicuous markings to further entice and guide the creatures that assist in pollination. When plant breeders select occasionally occurring sports and/or deliberately hybridize the plants to make double-flowered varieties, the whole *raison d'être* of the plant is altered or (in some cases) taken away. As far as I am concerned that blows away most of the pleasure of having the plant in my garden. How must a plant react when it has had its vital organs turned into a frivolity just to pleasure us humans? How disappointing and frustrating for the insects looking for a useful floral body part with which to interact. If a stamen is sacrificed and transposed into a comparatively dysfunctional petal, there is really no point in looking seductive! There is nothing to reward the pollinating insects, which would normally gather pollen and nectar in return for their services. Indeed, we do some very strange things to plants. Sometimes scent is sacrificed in the cause of altering or perfecting a colour or, worse still, to make a plant "dwarf" and thereby distort its proportions, often in a grotesque way.

TRADITIONAL COTTAGE-GARDEN PLANTS I first referred to Margery Fish (see Useful Books, page 205) for a wider selection of cottage-garden plants than either my mother or my grandfather had grown in their gardens. Aquilegias, phloxes, delphiniums, lupins and poppies were first to spring to mind when I thought back to the halcyon days when, as a "child-gardener", everything in the garden was simple and, yes, rosy. It is fruitless to try and categorize cottage-garden plants, herbs and wildflowers separately because they usually borrow some of each other's credentials. Country folk relied on the common sense and knowledge handed down through generations and most of their garden space would be taken up with edible plants and herbs. They probably had no need to prioritize wildlife-friendly plants; the need for premeditated conservation had yet to arrive. To make sure of pollination and to supplement their diet they or their neighbours probably kept honey-bees. I bore some of the folk history of artisan garden-making in mind during the gestation period between the conception and the delivery of my infant garden. I am by no means a compulsive collector of plants but I developed a penchant for geraniums and there are many varieties in this garden, as well as in each of the others.

CONSTRUCTION

Before any of my dreams could begin to become a reality there was some very serious groundwork to undertake. So, to begin at the beginning: it was 1988 when we began the daunting task of setting out and cultivating the 37m- (40yd-) diameter Round Garden.

I ran a line from the centre of my French windows to the appointed spot to the south and marked it. I then stuck a stout stake at the exact point in the middle and attached to it a 40m (43yd) length of string. Using this simple giant compass, I measured and marked out the concentric rings with ever-widening distances between them, like a ripple of water in the ocean of the existing rough, but very closely scalped, grass. I used farm-animal marker-dye to trace the exact pattern and gave myself a couple of weeks to try out the routes I had mapped to make sure they would work in a fluid and workable way as part of our daily beat around our property. After all, this was a pivotal point in the main passage to the most regularly visited parts of our land – the hen-run and the stockyard, on the eastern and south-western edges, respectively.

Once I had made the definitive adjustments, Peter and I began the gargantuan task of hand-digging, manuring and forming the beds. We removed the topsoil from the paths, where it was not needed, and added it to the beds to increase their height to

A desolate scene indeed! We certainly had to focus hard on our ultimate vision as we struggled with the layout and preparation of paths, borders and railway-sleeper steps during the cold winter of 1987.

provide better drainage and increase their potential for growing healthy plants. We double-dug each bed in order to bury the top layer of turf to a level where grasses and weeds would be devoid of light and so die off and decompose to make much-needed humus. The many tons of well-rotted farmyard manure (which we added) would help in this respect and put lost vitality back into the soil. In this part of our land, the ground had not been cultivated for many years but, even so, the quantity of our beautiful loamy topsoil above the subsoil varied considerably from place to place and we took this into account when redistributing the topsoil from the paths.

The drainage system had to be sensitively installed at the same time; it ran diagonally across the whole site beneath one of the dissecting paths, making it easy to locate and tap into in case we needed to access it in the future. By doing the work by hand we were able to avoid the unworkable quagmire that we found in the Frog Garden. Treating soil with utmost respect is fundamental to successful garden-making.

MAKING THE PATHS   In my dreams I would like to have constructed the paths using a variety of materials, to form the intricate pattern of a knot garden. In that way I could have achieved the spirit of an elaborate Elizabethan creation without torturing plants to form symbolic and decorative interwoven designs. In the harsh reality of our finances, the circular and dissecting paths were constructed using a gloomy assortment of broken, recycled paving slabs, which we tendered for and bought at bargain price from the local council. We needed a low-cost, sound base to make sure the paths would take the wear and tear in the years ahead so we laid them in a random pattern but used the largest pieces in the centre of the path to carry the load. I reckoned that looking at yard upon yard of sub-standard crazy-paving would drive us to distraction and be a nightmare to maintain, so it was always our intention to splash-out and cover the dizzy-making base with gravel.

We used path gravel or "hogging" as a first coating because this rugged sand/stone mixture consolidates well, especially if rolled when damp and left for a few days to set. Later on, when all the preparations were complete and the first stage of the planting had begun, we invested in expensive 6mm (¼ in) gravel and I topped the surface of the inner paths to look smart and reflect the heat of the sun. This

Dreams came true just a few years on as the garden gradually matured and the carefully selected and orchestrated plants began to weave their spell-binding magic.

surface provides extra warmth for the plants and a place for the butterflies to bask and (I have been told) from which to draw minerals. The gravelled paths are fully exposed to the sun because the planting in this central area of the design is no more than half a metre (18in) tall. The planting height then gradually ascends towards the outer beds where the tallest nectar plants rise to about 2m (6ft) in places. Here the outer paths remained more rugged-looking with just the hogging and, for a while, I enjoyed the visual contrast of texture and the slight difference underfoot. After a few years, the harsh sound and the feel of the paths began to grate on my nerves. I knew just how bad it was when a visiting BBC *Gardener's World* film crew asked us to drag out our carpets to muffle the sound while they were trying to make a programme on the pleasures of butterfly gardening! By then the garden was maturing rapidly and we had quantities of woody prunings to shred, so I began to smother the paths on the outer ring with this recycled garden debris. This had the triple effect of suppressing the annoying growth of weeds and of giving me the softness and quietness I desired, as well as the ability to wildlife-watch with more stealth, so enabling me to get closer to the shyer species.

The new system also impacted on wildlife. The butterflies still had their warm, central, gravelled paths but on the outer circle, as the shredding decomposed, the bark paths became a perfect habitat for worms to work and subsequently became a first-class hunting ground for birds. OK, so they scratched the bark all over the place but what the hell – they were effectively mulching the edges of the beds and saving me the chore! Every year we top up the supply with an increasing quantity of shreddings.

We had made no futile investment in an underlay of horticultural fabric between the soil and the surface materials. No invasive, perennial weeds were likely to resurrect from the barren subsoil and this type of membrane does nothing to prevent weeds germinating on the surface of gravel or bark topping. The birds make a good job of "hoeing" the bark paths and keeping them reasonably free of weeds, but the gravel paths are much more labour-intensive. I share the workload between my worn fingers and bent back plus an occasional bout with a flame-thrower.

PLANTING

Bearing in mind the importance of my enclosing hedgerows, I added both woody and herbaceous native species to build on the range I had inherited in my splendid hedge.

Brambles join a bed of similarly rampant but valuable wildlife plants safely contained in their own jungle border and merging into the boundary hedgerow.

The beautiful butter-coloured Brimstone butterfly is just as choosy as Hairstreaks when it searches for a maternity unit; only purging buckthorn (chalky soil) or alder buckthorn (acid soil) will do. Neither buckthorns existed anywhere in my hedgerows so, having neutral soil, I added several plants of both species wherever I had a sunny enough aspect to satisfy the female Brimstone's exact habitat specifications. Thank heavens Brimstones are less picky with their adult diet than the one upon which they insist for their offspring – though thistles are their preferred nectar plant.

Not surprisingly, I did not have to plant extra brambles! I just had to tolerate and lightly control their prickly, rambling ways so that they could continue to be great providers of nectar and berries without our falling out with each other. Their nectar contains three sorts of sugar so I guess that makes them triply nourishing for insects. One of the best ways to control a thuggish plant is to pitch a few more bullies into the ring and I am lucky to have sufficient space to allow a battle-royal to rage in a few appointed spots. My contenders include rosebay willowherb and campion, the food plants for the Elephant Hawk-moth and the Campion moth, respectively.

In this stretch of hedgerow I have allowed in aromatic herbs such as mint, lemon balm and tansy, all of which act like hooligans in the garden borders but ooze nectar and, as a result, are a magnet for insects. Aromatic foliage can often act as an insect deterrent but perhaps the leaves have to be disturbed to trigger the release of the natural chemicals that have this effect. Mint beetles obviously haven't been told about it because these spectacular metallic-green insects devour mint leaves like locusts. As all gardeners know, mint has unparalleled powers of recovery, so it suffers no ill effect from playing host to a most intriguing insect.

EXPERIMENTAL PLANTING It was to be several years before I was able to acquire and propagate all the plants I needed to begin to bring the complex and ever-evolving planting design into fruition. But, in the meantime, I made an interesting start and used vegetables and colour-selected annuals as infill, rather like an under-coat for the paintwork. Somehow I needed to cover as much bare earth as possible to stifle the weed growth and minimize the erosion of soil and loss of water by evaporation. In this respect, hand weeding, rather than hoeing, was the order of the day (in fact, most days, to begin with). Carefully measured weed tolerance is just fine in mature borders but in the formative year or so of a newly composed planting I am a strict disciplinarian. This plant-gathering time presented a great opportunity to study a vast range of mostly perennial plants, including many herbs and grasses, and to begin to learn exactly how to mix, match and blend the colours. I use the word "begin" advisedly; there is an unlimited journey of discovery because the possibilities and permutations are endless.

INSECT-WORTHINESS During the process we also began to discover which were the prime nectar plants. It was particularly interesting to observe how the bees and butterflies became complacent about a favoured plant once they discovered a new one they liked better. For instance, the first year the Small Tortoiseshell butterflies flocked around my anise hyssop (*Agastache rugosa*) to such an extent that they caused me an abrupt "double take" because I thought for a moment I had mistakenly planted an orange plant among the subtle the purple, lavender and lilac combination I was composing! By the following year I had planted several varieties of scabious and the fickle Tortoiseshells forsook the anise hyssop almost completely. I was comforted to see that the bees remained true to their opinion that the plant is indeed nectar-worthy. It seems bees were easier to please.

EARLIEST NECTAR PLANTS The majority of the very earliest nectar-producing plants in my garden grow in my nearby woodland garden and in other sheltered

Reading across, from top left: *Echinacea purpurea* is a magnet for Tortoiseshell and several other butterfly species; a ladybird forages amongst the awns of the barley grass; spiky *Liatris spicata* tempts the Brimstone butterfly; alliums such as *A. sphaerocephalon* are favoured by bees and hoverflies; Mint beetles devour and help restrain the spread of mint; the Comma butterfly nectars on purple loosestrife; late-summer asters are a feast for late hatchings of Red Admirals; a Speckled Wood ventures onto *Angelica gigas*.

spots where snowdrops, hellebores, primroses, comfrey and pulmonarias are more suitably placed. I have very few bulbs in the Round Garden because they complicate the process of managing herbaceous plants and grasses, which need lifting and separating from time to time. Bulbs are wonderful for early nectar but I use them in places where they can remain undisturbed. However, some of these plants and bulbs stray into the perimeter of the Round Garden among the limited number of shrubs that grow in the outer circle. In natural habitats this could be compared to the more shaded edge of the woodland glade.

THE EARLY SCENE There is a sprinkling of biennial, self-seeding honesty dotted through the outer borders and hopefully making a breeding-ground for the early-flying Orange Tip butterflies and leaving an infiltration of beautiful silvery seed-heads for winter. Dame's violet (*Hesperis matronalis*) is also useful to Orange Tips so I provide a very attractive pale mauve one which blends with my plant colours. *Allium hollandicum* 'Purple Sensation' matches well and grows willingly, the first of several I include for bees' delight. Aquilegias are one of the first plants to have stirred a deep passion in my heart and each year this emotion is rekindled when they appear in shades of mulberry, pink, mauve, purple and lavender-blue in almost the places I had in mind.

Some plants have a will of their own and it is counter-productive to try and argue the case for a strict colour discipline. I used to try but no longer do. Soon the whole scene is dominated by shell-pink valerian which also grows mostly in the larger beds towards the outer ring. This is the real thing – *Valeriana officinalis* – with calming herbal properties and a soothing appearance. It is a native plant which stands about 1 to 1.2m (3 to 4ft) tall on strong stems (not to be confused with *Centranthus ruber*, the "wall" valerian, which is unrelated). Visitors often think it is a pink form of *Verbena bonariensis* and are understandably confused by the similarities of form. To a lesser degree it is also a "see-through" plant and it does have verbena-like flat heads. It differs in having an elusive scent which is usually pleasing but at times appears strangely disagreeable. Herbs and wildflowers are always full of mystery, which is probably why I love them, especially when they are as pretty and useful as valerian.

Early summer in the Round Garden and a haze of cloud grass fringes the camomile lawn. The multitude of nectar-rich plants generate a constant buzz and flutter as beneficial insects are drawn to our sunny, sheltered glade.

It continues to impress for weeks because, as the flowers fade, the fluffy seed-heads remain a modest feature for us, are of continued interest to insects and finches keenly eat the seeds. This valerian has fairly attractive foliage, is totally hardy, self-supporting, self-seeds willingly, transplants uncomplainingly, prefers damp ground but tolerates dryish conditions and will compete quite well in grass (its natural habitat). Sometimes it isn't necessary for plant-finders to travel to the ends of the earth to find a good plant; it can be right under your nose.

Towards the centre of my "sunny glade" *Allium cristophii* is among the few bulbs planted and is one of the earliest of the nectar-rich flowers. The starry globes are set in a silvery sea of grasses, including my beloved cloud grass. There is some dispute whether this annual grass is *Agrostis nebulosa* or *Aira elegantissima*. I sit on the botanical fence and just admire. Who minds? It is just exquisite and never more so than when glittering with dew or raindrops, which it holds like millions of tiny sparkling diamonds. In June its young flowers are silvery green, then become quite a feisty

pink during July before holding on in a more modest buff colour until about October. Foxtail barley grass (*Hordeum jubatum*) comes into action as the cloud grass is fading and, if dead-headed, flowers until November unless struck down by frost.

Scabious, marjoram, thyme and prunellas are very fine nectar providers. Marjoram, above all other plants, is beloved by the Gatekeepers, Meadow Browns and Common Blues, which are more often found in my meadows but breeze in to the Round Garden when nectar stocks begin to diminish a little in the grassland. I grow the finely foliaged, aromatic, silver-leafed *Artemisia canescens* for my own pleasure and for the ladybirds which very often inhabit it. By autumn, the innocent sounding (but somewhat over-domineering) *Festuca mariei* takes control of the inner ring. This large festuca has fine, grey-green, gently arching foliage and just a scattering of slender flowering stems that stand at twice the height of the foliage. But by autumn, small plants have gradually become dense tussocks; a wonderful habitat for insects but a bit overwhelming for its more frail bedfellows.

HARDY GERANIUMS Having disclaimed myself as a plantaholic I do seem to have amassed a fair collection of geraniums. All of my species and varieties are very tough and amenable, extremely attractive to bees and some have seeds which the finches eat with relish. I believe the phaeum types are best in both respects. *Geranium phaeum* 'Lily Lovell', for example, behaves true to form and has very lovely violet-coloured

Globes of *Allium cristophii* set amongst a silvery sea of early cloud grass. A week or two later the same grass assumes a shimmering pink glow.

flowers that are larger than those of my other phaeums, in shades of palest pink to deepest plummy maroon colours. *Geranium pratense* is dear to me because it is a wildflower of our meadows, which is where I confine the true species. This garden is a stud farm for some of the lovely chance progeny to further interbreed. Some very subtle-coloured descendants are emerging including my 'Blue Shimmer' (see Frog Garden) and others we will meet. *Geranium sylvaticum* is another native that I grow extensively, but it is white, and white plants are excluded from the Round Garden because they can be over-conspicuous. I just allow the violet-mauve, white-centred *G. s.* 'Mayflower' into this particular arena. The third native geranium species is *Geranium sanguineum*, whose purple-magenta colour fits perfectly with the scheme of colours at their most extreme range. *Geranium sanguineum var. striatum* has barely a trace of that colouring in its gentle, light pink flowers. The sanguineums have neat, finely divided foliage that often colours well in autumn. *Geranium maculatum* grows wild in moist meadows and woodland in North America. It has quite large, soft mauve flowers early in the season and then the plant sits good-naturedly tucked away, swallowed up in the exuberant growth of later-flowering perennials. *Geranium* 'Johnson's Blue' is the bluest of my collection, lacking the violet veining that tints some of the other purple-blues such as those of *Geranium ibericum*, *G. himalayense* and *G. x magnificum* which intensify in colour, ascending in that order. Amongst the redder-purple assortment, *Geranium x oxonianum f. thurstonianum* is a great rambling creature which means business; as an efficient, ground-covering individual it is best given space to get on with it. This way it will continue an extended flowering period as it progresses, arm over arm, to make new flowering growth on top of the original. Its flowers have oddly shaped, narrow, pointed, petals. My most intensively livid magenta is *Geranium psilostemon*, which glowers passionately with its dark eyes. *Geranium psilostemon* 'Bressingham Flair' is a blink or two less dynamic and *G. clarkei* 'Kashmir Purple' has none of that dazzling, day-glow element. Wide-eyed and innocent-looking, *G.c.* 'Kashmir White' is a stunner that likes to gaze at the sun and turns its head to do so. It is made the palest of pinks by the colour of the fine web of lilac veins on white petals. Both Kashmirs have a busy root system and a deceptively lively habit of gaining territory and smothering their neighbours.

Similarly tinged pink, *Geranium x cantabrigiense* 'Biokovo' is far less rampant and my favourite of the smaller macrorrhizum dynasty, having the aromatic foliage of its brethren but a much neater habit. *Geranium x cantabrigiense* is a magenta-pink and *G. macrorrhizum* 'Bevan's Variety' is a shade or two more intense, but neither of these become over-intrusive. The earliest geraniums start to flower in May and, with some mid-season dead-heading, most continue for three or four months.

COHERENT COLOUR   After a fragmented start to the essentially mid- to late-summer planting compositions in the larger beds, the full palette of colours eventually manifests; they begin to flow from soft, pastel colours at the northern segment near the house to become richer and deeper southwards, where the crimson, violet and magenta zone attract the most insects towards the height of their season. Like a water-colour painting, the lavender-blues and palest yellows are washed in from the Frog Garden to the south west while the pinks and reds fuse in from the Bird Garden to the south east. This expands the feeling of circularity to encompass all three of the gardens surrounding the house.

STRONG PINK BORDER, WITH RED COMPANIONS   The richest of pinks and maroons are arranged in the mixed border closest to the Bird Garden. The bed has a wealth of provision for wildlife; it includes fruit and seed-heads for birds but focuses mostly on insects, many of which will, in turn, become high-protein food for birds and other creatures in the food chain. This large bed contains *Malus* 'Wisley', which displays its sultry pink blossom against purple-tinged foliage and has huge, aubergine-coloured crab apples. Close by grows the complementary, claret-coloured *Berberis* 'Red Chief' with its dark berries and the needle-like thorns that help make it a safe roosting or nesting place for birds. Nearby, and suckering merrily into its neighbours, the good-natured, crimson-maroon rose 'Tuscany' makes a decorative thicket and tolerates the same-coloured *Knautia macedonica* thrusting its way among its stems and adding small, embossed, deep red dots to the larger, flat heads of the velvety rose. I clear just a few of the suckers to leave space for my annual opium

A close community of nectar-rich cottage-garden plants that include *Allium sphaerocephalon*, *Liatris spicata*, *Knautia macedonica*, nicotiana, our own *Eryngium* 'Bewitched' and an accidentally double opium poppy.

poppies, *Papaver somniferum*, which are nothing like as well able to compete where space is in dispute. Time spent in this necessary intervention is well worthwhile when it results in the unparalleled joy of managing to grow my exquisite fimbriated poppy, the colour of blackcurrant jam. I envy the seemingly ecstatic bees as they tumble about in the jungle of golden, pollen-dusted stamens.

How amazing to belong, and be essential to, a world of flowers and to be able to fly from one to another, lured in by their colours, scent, shapes and patterns – all the features which make them fascinating to us as mere onlookers. At the back of this group stands the tallest and the most productive of my nectar-yielding perennials, which is just about equal in popularity with buddleia in this respect. It has large, silky, dusky-purplish-pink flower-heads that are just slightly dome-shaped. Over 1.5m (5ft) in height, yet self-supporting, *Eupatorium purpureum* is truly magnificent looking. Even into deepest winter, its stately stems and seed-heads persist, the assembled plants looking like a diminutive, skeletal rainforest. It is

closely related to *Eupatorium cannabinum* or hemp agrimony – a wildflower belonging in damp meadows.

THE BORDER BECOMES PALER ...   Set against a backdrop of the impressive grass, *Miscanthus sinensis malepartus*, and the similar but slightly shorter *M. sinensis* 'Rotsilber', together with fluffy pink *Filipendula rubra*, there is *Lupinus* 'My Castle', *Echinacea purpurea*, *Persicaria amplicaulis* 'Atrosanguinea' and *Leonurus cardiaca*, which are all very well-endowed with nectar. Admittedly, I rarely see a butterfly on the persicaria; the usual pollinators are wasps and sometimes hoverflies, so I was astonished when I found a Holly Blue nectaring on the red flower-spikes. Both bees and butterflies adore echinacea, which attracts the Tortoiseshells, Red Admirals, Commas and even Clouded Yellows – less often found in gardens as visiting migrants. They list sideways, oddly, to expose their wings to the right angle to gain maximum heat from the sun. As flight is their means of travelling great distances and escaping from predators, they have to keep their wings in first-class working order.

I often wonder if insects recognize the herbal properties of plants like echinacea, which is well-recognized for its ability to boost the immune system. Large

bumblebees have the strength to force open the jaws of the pink lupin with its evocative, peppery scent; a scent which transports me back in time to my grandfather's garden and my earliest memories of, and association with, gardens. There is a luscious, similarly coloured, pink opium poppy with a maroon blotch at its base helping to keep the purple-pink colours threading through the border. Sometimes I succeed in helping a crop of dark, purple-podded French beans to romp towards the back of the border and add a little *je ne sais quoi* to the composition. *Leonurus cardiaca*, or "motherwort", has an easy clue to its medicinal virtues in both the Latin and the folk name. It is a little-grown herb, probably because its subdued pink flower colour is so modest and because modern mothers seem to be strangely mistrustful of ancient "witchcraft" to ease the pain of childbirth, placing more confidence in modern drugs. However, I am devoted to it because it is an obliging, self-seeding, self-supporting "vertical" with an outstandingly long-lasting and impressive seed-head and strong, square, hollow stems that eventually become excellent insect breeding sites.

Two very special wildflowers grow in the bed nearby. Ragged Robin (*Lychnis flos-jovis*) is now as rare in the wild as it is abundant at Sticky Wicket. It seeds itself in a well-balanced matrix among *Achillea* 'Apfelblute' (formerly 'Apple Blossom') and *A. millefolium* 'Cerise Queen'. This interests me because these plants are naturally occurring bedfellows in meadows (damp ones) where ragged Robin cohabits with *Achillea millefolium*, or yarrow. Spiny restharrow (*Ononis spinosa*) is another very garden-worthy native plant. It prefers drier, chalky ground but defies the predicted science and copes well enough perched on one of the steeper edges of my winter-wet flower bed. It is covered in sprays of small, pink, pea-like flowers that make a decorative edging and please the bees at the same time.

There is an even softer pink planting close by with the paler pinks easing the way back to the mixture of pastel colours in front of the house where I wanted a minimal colour impact. *Lythrum salicaria* 'Blush' is a variety of our native loosestrife and has two-toned, pink flower spikes that help to graduate the flow. *Veronicastrum virginicum roseum* – a magnet for bees – is taller and more elegant with slender, pale-pink spires

The fluffy flower heads of *Filipendula rubra* 'Venusta' in the background and the pink astilbe to the fore make a soft background for the spikes and spires of *Lupinus* 'My Castle' beloved by bumblebees, *Lythrum* 'Blush' and the herb, motherwort.

that stand firm and imposing with rich, cinnamon-brown winter seed-heads.

I wanted a very pale pink umbelliferous flower to complement the veronicastrum and the grasses that accompany it. I chose coriander as a perfect companion. It is an annual herb that always seems to be in a hurry to flower and make seed rather than produce tasty foliage. I decided to let it have its way and I enjoy both seeing the results and eating the seeds instead of the leaves. Soapwort (*Saponaria officinalis*) is a herb with a sweet fragrance which attracts moths. I grow it in one of the smallest beds – partly as a ploy to contain it in a relatively small space. Beautiful it may be, but "thuggish" would be a civil word to describe the way it behaves in company. I would never want to be without it, but it is worth thinking long and hard before setting it loose in polite society. I have difficulty in restraining the pernicious root system from penetrating the neighbouring assembly which includes *Oenothera speciosa* 'Siskiyou', nestling into a soft haze of *Stipa tenuissima*. Only a little human intervention is required to sustain a meadow-like balance between the two because both are inveterate self-seeders. However, I tamper with the grass and thin the flowering stems from time to time to control the tangle of growth that can inhibit its ability to wave in the breeze.

MOTH APPEAL   As well as soapwort, moths are attracted to evening primroses. I wonder if pink ones work for them or is it the yellow colouring that is the criteria? There is still a whole world of night-life to discover including the mysterious world of bats which I sometimes see insect-hunting at dusk. I grow several varieties of honeysuckle on the perimeter of this garden because I believe moths particularly favour this plant and I can smell why. As I also adore it, there is certainly no hardship involved in allowing *Lonicera periclymenum* 'Belgica' to intertwine among mature shrubs such as *Escalonia* 'Apple Blossom', which also happens to be a good source of nectar. I cannot put a name to the nearby seedling hebe that arrived by chance just when I had given up the struggle to grow named varieties on the comparatively exposed site during the early years. This vagrant hebe is tough and surprisingly tolerant of my soggy soil conditions.

PALE PINK, PALE YELLOW AND PALE LAVENDER   These are by no means a fashionable mix of colours but they are an essential part of my planting strategy to accommodate all the plants in my brief, while achieving the gentle progression of colours I wanted. To make a butterfly and bee paradise I obviously needed to include several buddleias which I intended to grow in a range of colours to match each part of the circle. *Buddleia fallowiana* has grey foliage and the palest, rather ghostly lavender-mauve flower-spike, similar to B. 'Lochinch', but just a little more refined. I have two other plants in the same class which grow nearby. One, an uncertified delphinium, is slightly paler with greyish undertones and just the slightest hint of yellow. The individual flowers are delightfully uncrowded on stems which benefit from only a little necessary support. I love this plant dearly and call this delphinium 'Dodie' after the local lady who kindly gave it to me. It survives with absolutely no measures to control slugs, seems to come true from seed and, unlike other delphs I have tried to grow, it is a real trooper. I have an iris which, strangely enough, happens to have exactly the same elements in its colour make-up. I brought it with me from my last home and although its name has slipped my mind, its fabulous fragrance is totally unforgettable.

By some sort of magical chance interbreeding among my meadow geraniums,

Planting for wildlife need never be at the expense of aesthetics! The vertical form of veronica contrasts with soft, flowing barley grass; they are a perfect partnership in colour and both plants have value for the insect population.

Geranium 'Dove' emerged nearby and I soon adopted it and named it thus to reflect the gentleness of its subtle colouring (just a shade paler than the delphinium) and because it grows near Aster 'Ring Dove'. This tiny-flowered aster performs in autumn, when the geranium finally gives up after two rounds. The minute daisy flowers of the aster give it a hazy look – as if it is permanently surrounded in its own romantic autumn mist. Calamintha nepeta also looks as if it has partially materialized out of a morning mist, although in all probability one might hear this plant before seeing it! There are few plants which create such a buzz among bees of all sorts. Even in dense fog or darkness you could trace its whereabouts by the delicious minty aroma of its minuscule leaves. And should you, perchance, be groping about in the darkness, Stachys byzantina (syn. S. lanata) is also an interesting plant to encounter. Its common name, "lamb's ears", tells you it has the softest of foliage and although the flower stems look similarly textured, they are really unexpectedly harsh. I think it must be this feature which enables bumblebees to cling on to the pale lilac flowers when they

are braving out the summer rains. (They use eryngiums in the same way.) Stachys shares the ghostly and nectar-producing qualities with the calamintha.

PALE PINK MEETS PALE YELLOW   Maybe *Rosa* 'Lucetta' (syn. *R.* 'Ausemi') is not actually the palest of the David Austin roses but it is one of the healthiest I have met and this tall shrub is a good shape. The old-fashioned, cabbage-shaped flowers are deeply scented, not disproportionately over-large and have the grace to just about show their yellow stamens enough to make me feel they are not entirely dysfunctional for all wildlife. With regular dead-heading and the benefit of my top-grade garden compost, 'Lucetta''s flowering season lasts into October. They then look marvellous against the neighbouring miscanthus when it displays silky, pink, tassel-like flowers at this time. 'Lykkefund' is also a pink rose and there, apart from a similarly hearty constitution, the similarities end. It is a climbing rose, conveniently thornless, and has virtually no scent but is most prettily smothered in masses of small, loosely double blooms which have the same subtle yellow under-tones that somehow allow it to combine with the delphinium in the most pleasing but unlikely way. *Hemerocallis* 'Catherine Woodberry' helps link the colours because her soft pink flowers have a hint of yellow to remind her of her ancestry. Other yellows come from the pale *Oenothera odorata* whose spent flowers then conveniently fade to pink. This allows me to cue-in two of my favourite grasses; foxtail barley grass (described in Bird Garden) and *Calamagrostis brachytricha* whose squirrel tail plumes have a pink phase as well as a silver one. Fennel is a stronger yellow with no trace of any other colour but the ample helping of finely divided green foliage tones it down and allows it to be a wonderful mixer in a border where yellow appears. It is another herb which insects, including hoverflies, love to visit for nectar. I am happy to allow it to self-seed amongst all the plants in the group but now and again I dig up some of the older plants if they are in the way or I may just thin out the odd flowering stems (and live on a generous diet of well-flavoured fish and fennel tea for a day or two). This border relates to the western side of the Round Garden where there is a visual connection to the Frog Garden but the lavender-lilac-blue colouring

The Round Garden in the mid-90s as the character of the garden continued to evolve; at this stage, Mediterranean shrubs were still surviving the increasingly wet winters and annuals, such as nicotiana, featured more conspicuously.

intensifies as the planting progresses towards the southern zone at the top, where we sit looking back towards the house.

DEVELOPING THE PURPLE HAZE   There is a seat set in a metal-framed, willow-woven arbour which is home to a divinely scented, annual, bicoloured sweet pea, *Lathyrus odorata*. If there is a rare moment to spare, it is here that we sit, having a cup of tea and watching the butterflies on the plant groups in shades of lavender, mauve, violet and magenta which are picked up in the sweet pea and its accompanying *Clematis* 'Kermesina'. These colours are sometimes difficult to describe but their combined effect can be loosely termed "purple" and, looking up from the house to the top of the Round Garden, I now see the purple haze I envisaged in 1988.

THE UBIQUITOUS BUDDLEIAS   A sequence of buddleias is "top totty" for the insects that visit a butterfly garden. *Buddleia alternifolia* flowers ahead of the rest in June

and I have known it to be absolutely covered in early-arriving Painted Ladies. I prune most buddleias very hard to ensure they flower a little later and so are timed for late summer when most butterflies are present. I leave one or two unpruned for earlier insects but these are the vagabond plants that set seed around the nursery where it matters not one jot how woody, overgrown and uncouth-looking they become.

Back in the garden, I also grow the special Buddleia 'Beijing', given to me by a butterfly conservationist and plant collector friend who realized it flowers a whole month later than any we commonly grow here and is perfectly timed for the late-hatching residents or late-arriving migrants. Professor David Bellamy recognized the importance of the introduction of this plant and has been promoting it nationwide. Among a host of others, I love to see Commas nectaring on this buddleia and on the similarly coloured B. 'Lochinch', their orange colour picked up in the eye of each of the mauve florets. It is said that butterflies prefer mauve buddleias but I have never noticed them turn up their noses (or probosces) at any of the other coloured buddleias such as B. 'Nanho Purple', 'Nanho Blue' or 'Black Knight'.

THE "LINEAR LOOK"   Starting with vervain, the plant that makes the least impact, I mention *Verbena officinalis* with a word of caution: its seeding habits can be tedious. I readily forgive it because it contains properties to staunch bleeding and cure infection – always handy – and prevent spells. (This may be a good precaution in a mystical space where any old witch could pass through unnoticed!) Vervain is a skinny individual with small leaves and very tiny pale lilac flowers at the tip of its slender stems. Little wonder it is not widely sought-after at garden centres but John Brookes used to tell us to use "not too much meat and add plenty of gravy" when selecting plants. How right he was: star plants need a more modest supporting cast. *Verbena hastata* is much taller with a slender, deeper-coloured, tapered flower-head. It has very greedy roots but at least they give good anchorage to the strong, self-supporting stems. *Teucrium hircanicum* is of medium height, and more floriferous, but still a quietly understated, pale violet spire. Bees like it but butterflies are indifferent. Anise hyssop (*Agastache foeniculum*) is a similar colour and texture and makes a slightly

Both my insects and I are especially attracted to the violet spectrum of plants. Among the assembled August-flowering plants there are various buddleias, monardas and phloxes, interspersed with *Verbena bonariensis*.

more substantial impact. It is a herb with a pleasing aniseed aroma and I sometimes put a few leaves in salad or dry a few for my homemade pot-pourri. Both bees and butterflies are attracted to the agastache's chunky flower spikes. It is not a long-lived perennial but easy to grow from seed.

Even more impressive are the taller spikes of *Liatris spicata*, or "gay feather" to address it more familiarly! The bright, purple-magenta spikes broaden at the top and the plant makes an impact which merits positioning it so it can, indeed, steal the show for a few weeks. The stage is then well set for the arrival of the ultimate adornment – the butterflies. Last year the liatris chiefly took the fancy of Brimstones and Clouded Yellows and the combination of plant and insects was simply mesmerizing.

Nepeta racemosa and the smaller N. x *faassenii* have spiked flower heads but the plant has a floppy manner of growth with a soft appearance that barely makes an impression on my linear-look objectives. However, both bees and butterflies love this plant and so do silver "Y" moths. These day-flying moths are wonderfully fluttery, grey-brown insects which visit a great range of plants but seem to highly favour blue flowers such as nepeta. Where there is limited space for *Nepeta* 'Six Hills Giant' to sprawl, I grow N. x *faassenii*. Although this plant is shorter and neater, it is less robust; over the years I believe many have perished on account of my soggy winter soil conditions. I believe *Nepeta* 'Souvenir d'André Chaudron' eventually met the same fate, although in its early years it seemed unstoppable as it ran amok through the newly dug borders with its more upright, soft, lavender-blue flower stems.

Astilbe 'Purple Lance' is a fine, tall plant with just the visual impact I seek. I have to mulch it well to help it to weather the dry spells in summer. I suppose the flower-heads are more of a plume than a spire or spike, but they enhance the effect I try to achieve as a 21st-century-garden "impressionist". If I have one grievance with astilbes it is this: their dead-heads are very fine but they occur too early in the year. I am ready and waiting for brown flowers after September but before that they look like a premature death, which has a depressing effect on the rest of the planting. Sometimes I stick it out but other times the twitchy secateur fingers become uncontrollable and I cheer myself up for the instant – but deprive the winter garden of a valued member for several months ahead.

The tallest of this sequence of spires is *Lythrum salicaria*, known as purple loosestrife: a colourful wildflower often found on river banks. The flowers, which are the same magenta/purple colour as the liatris, draw in scores of bees and butterflies. I find it is Brimstones and Commas which like it the most, but they certainly find more secretive places to roost. A predator could spot them a mile off and I do have a rather large and healthy population of birds! Even when I am ferreting about in the borders, I never find them loitering in odd places on dull days. They must disguise themselves well while they hang about waiting for a sunny moment to fly. I don't suppose they know how brilliant and beautiful they look against the vibrant flower colour but perhaps they realize they are highly conspicuous when feeding. I have planted one or two garden cultivars, such as *Lythrum virgatum* 'Dropmore Purple' and *L. salicaria* 'Firecandle', in my time but some skulduggery seems to have occurred. As a result I can detect some minimal colour variations in the ensuing generations but I cannot vouch for the pedigree of the offspring. I might be accused of allowing lythrum a little too much freedom of occupation in the garden but I also value this plant for its fine, upstanding, skeletal winter form. In spite of its tendency to seed itself rather liberally, I leave it standing until February or March and have months of pleasure admiring the tawny stems and seed-heads, especially with the grassy foliage of *Miscanthus sinensis* 'Gracillimus' arching gracefully among them. Both plants gleam in the rain and on frosty mornings they look outstanding when hoary-edged with white.

ROUND FLOWER-HEADS FOR CONTRAST I am often asked what my impressive, long-flowering, bee-attracting alliums are. There are looks of incredulity when I reply, "They are leeks.". I love to mix edible plants into the borders, especially when they look so fine and function so well as a wildlife attractor. The decorative effect of leeks is superbly complementary to *Salvia sclarea* var. *turkestanica*, or clary sage in herbal parlance. They share the same mixture of almost indefinable pallid pink and ashen-mauve colouring, although their shape and form are totally contrasting. The salvia seeds can be soaked in water to make a soothing eyewash – therefore quite a pertinent companion to an onion. It certainly is a "sight for sore eyes" – as they say – although the aroma is an acquired taste. Bergamot is another herb that bees frequent and butterflies sometimes visit. I grow a variety called *Monarda* 'Blue Stocking', which is actually a strong magenta colour. It has quite strange "mop-heads" with long, arched flower tubes. Its seed-heads last for months and look particularly impressive when iced with frost. Salsify is a wonderfully decorative vegetable; so much so I seldom eat it. It is related to *Tragopogon pratensis*, known as goat's beard and also Jack-go-to-bed-at-noon. Like its wild yellow relative, salsify's soft, round, lilac flowers close up at noon but the extra-large dandelion-clock seed-heads and even the pointed, closed heads lend a distinct touch of drama.

SCABIOUS TYPES   Of all my ace nectar plants, I think scabious make the most perfectly enchanting platform for butterflies to display their beauty as they delicately sip the sugary juices. Large-flowered varieties such as *Scabiosa caucasica* are certainly very decorative but all the charming floral details exist in the smaller, wild species and it is these that I prefer to grow. They also happen to survive much better in my damp, clay soil. *Scabiosa columbaria* is very branched with masses of small, lavender-blue flowers that are often covered in a crowd of predominantly Small Tortoiseshell butterflies which also like the devil's-bit scabious (*Succisa pratensis*). This wildflower loves to grow in damp meadows or on chalk so perhaps it is this versatility that helps it to excel as a garden plant. The stems are less branched than the former scabious and the pin-head flowers a little deeper-coloured. Devil's-bit is the specific food plant of the rare Marsh Fritillary, but the chances of one visiting are fairly slim in most gardens, mine included. They need a traditionally managed woodland environment where their caterpillar food plant, violets, can proliferate. However, the usual garden butterflies and the bees will be just as happy as I am with the devil's bit. Common knapweed (*Centaurea nigra*) is another admirable wildlife-attracting wildflower that will enthusiastically adapt to garden conditions and I have selected and propagated some very fine specimens from those growing in my meadow. The colours and forms can be variable and I have singled out the later-flowering ones with the most exaggerated rays and the richest colours, from mauve to magenta. This has pleased a wide range of butterflies as well as bees, hoverflies and Burnet Moths. The garden knapweed (*Centaurea montana*) flowers earlier in the year and is also a good nectar plant. I have pink, blue and purple forms; all pretty-looking and all pretty mildew-ridden by mid-summer. They crowd themselves out with volumes of over-exuberant growth but I would rather forgive that trait than have to coax the reluctant

I love to integrate herbs and edible plants in my borders. Leeks are irresistible to bees and hoverflies, have long lasting, decorative flowers and seed-heads, and make handsome bedfellows for the clary sage (*Salvia sclarea* 'Turkestanica')

or faint-hearted one. Both native and garden knapweeds benefit from having the faded flower stems cut to the base to stimulate growth of fresh ones.

POTENTIALLY POTENT   The mauve-to-plum mix of colours of the lovely *Papaver somniferum*, far from having a soporific effect on bees, as the Latin name implies, sends them into a pollen-foraging frenzy! Growing "opium" could be said to put a little controversy into the planting associations. However, there are no dodgy substances in the seeds – they are quite safe to use for bread topping. Like many herbs, true opium (the garden one is not used in commercial production of the drug) is a valuable panacea in small doses, but becomes a dangerously addictive drug when abused. Nature probably provides us with most of the remedies we need to heal ourselves but we unfailingly upset the balance of power and abuse the gifts. (Imagine what havoc could result from modern genetic manipulation if the results are as unpredictable as some scientists suggest. Supposing important, undiscovered healing properties were to be lost in the process or as a result of unintended hybridization between GM and non-GM plants? And what if toxic properties were to manifest in an unforeseen way? "Scary" is the popular word to describe what I feel about the way this technology is being railroaded upon the environment before our plants and their potential powers are fully scientifically explored and recorded.)

FLATTISH HEADS   The elegant, see-through plant, *Verbena bonariensis*, is another superlative, late-flowering nectar plant. Its flower-heads make an ideal podium for butterflies including the stunning Painted Ladies whose pinkish-orange, patterned underwings are such a perfect study. Lovable little bumblebees also pose delightfully on the purple verbena, which appears to have been purposefully designed to display its pollinators at work. *Achillea millefolium* 'Lilac Queen' is dear to me because it is a close cousin to the grassland wildflower, yarrow. In spite of its name, it is distinctly pink but intermingles smoothly with another of my more flat-headed plants, *Phlox paniculata* 'Franz Schubert'. This is a good plant of medium height and bears flowers with a gentle merging of mauve-pink and white. It is floriferous to the point of embarrassment when trying to compose compositions where no one plant is over-dominant. I relieve the situation by prematurely dead-heading a proportion of the stems. The thinned clumps look more graciously elegant and the apparently cruelly treated stems then fully recover and flower again later, thus keeping the layered sequence going longer than it would otherwise. The same methods apply to *Phlox paniculata* 'Border Gem', whose fiery magenta colouring can be altogether a bit too show-stopping in a solid mass. I have another taller, unnamed and wilder-looking phlox that I much prefer to the aforementioned pair. This wildling's flowers are smaller, lilac-coloured and both the individual florets and the whole flower-heads are less cluttered and more neatly spaced than the hybrids. Because of its wilder provenance, I would like to be able to report that the insects prefer it to the modern hybrids but this is not apparent: rather the reverse, in fact.

Daisy flowers are also individually flat but, in the case of my asters, for example, are arranged in sprays. Asters are essential late-nectar stores for butterflies and I have two which I recommend for their beauty and disease-resistance. *Aster* 'September Charm' is a dark cerise-magenta which Red Admirals are glad to find at the end of the season. *Aster* 'Little Carlow' is violet-blue, extremely elegant and more valued by bees than butterflies. I would like to be able to champion 'Little Carlow' as an ace candidate for the wildlife garden because, as a garden-worthy plant, it is in a class above any other aster I have grown.

WILLIAM'S GROUP   The rose 'William Lobb' is a very beautiful dusky purple and crimson rose but has little to offer wildlife. However, it is a great treat for me and in amongst it there is a truly valuable collection of nectar plants, so I have singled out this group for special recommendation and will describe William's sequence of alluring bed-fellows. The honesty is first to flower, followed by our own star, the fabulous *Lupinus* 'Witchet'. 'Witchet' arrived as a seedling resulting from a cross between some old-fashioned lupins I grew from seed from an old cottage garden in Kent. Similar to L. 'Thundercloud', it is a thunderous purple, struck with the deep crimson flashes of its keel petals. *Cirsium rivulare* 'Atropurpureum's crimson, thistle-like flowers make a sumptuous place to hang out and feed if you are a bee. It begins to flower in May and if the faded stems are cut down, this plant will flower for months on end – even into December. Despite the rivulare bit, it grows in a range of conditions, provided it feels so inclined. I gather it can be a bit temperamental but so far it hasn't shown its teeth in my gardens. Corncockle, a wildflower now unhappily banished from cornfields, seems happy enough in my "border sanctuary". If I am lucky and the scattered seed germinates in the right place, it forms an impressive duet with the hardy *Salvia* 'Purple Rain' whose aspiring stems

Although the moss rose 'William Lobb' is beautiful and beguiling, it has no obvious attraction for wildlife. However, *Linaria purpurea* and *Lupinus* 'Witchet' (in the background) amply make up for the shortfall.

adds a desirable vertical element. The aster, well-named 'September Charm', flowers last of all just as the rugosa rosehips are ripening as a dual attraction for wildlife. I have great admiration for the mixture of tough rugosa roses that grow at the back of the border in question. The most highly scented and deepest crimson-coloured is 'Roseraie de l'Haye', which is semi-double with good hips, but there are also some more humble, single-flowered rugosas which the bees prefer. They all flower for ages, especially if dead-headed. Masses of insects visit for pollen and nectar and, when the hips form, there is food for birds, Red Admirals and field mice – and Pam Lewis, who also likes to nibble the vitamin C-rich flesh.

WEAVERS Leaving the last border with the bold clumps of nectar plants, you come to a small bed with a matrix of nectar plants weaving in among each other – more like the wildflowers of the meadow. *Knautia macedonica* has pretty, scabious-like flowers that grow in profusion on branching stems. Its colour range extends from deep crimson to pastel pink and mauve. They are constantly attended by wildlife, including bees, butterflies and then greenfinches, which feast greedily on the seeds. I have to restrain a little of the exuberance of the knautia, thinning out the oldest and tallest stems to persuade it not to overpower its bedfellows, in particular the less branching purple eryngium and the silvery-maroon *Allium sphaerocephalon*. The similar shape and "needlepoint" texture of this teasel-like pair makes it easy for the bumblebees to keep a firm grip and I find they often hang in there during rainstorms. Apart from the wildlife "underworld" that surrounds them, they make a sensational planting combination! The eryngium is seemingly unnamed because it developed as a reversion from a variegated form called 'Calypso', which seems to have disappeared from the current edition of the Plantfinder. The only clue to its parentage is that it looks like *Eryngium planum*, but the colour is more intensely purple so I have taken the liberty of naming it E. 'Bewitched'. Understandably my green-leafed plant, having escaped the restraints on its health relating to the variegation, seems much happier *au naturel*.

Oregano is a herb I often use in cooking and pot-pourri and is one of the top-of-the-range nectar plants. *Origanum laevigatum* 'Hopley's' is one of the tallest, finest-looking and richest coloured purple. *O. l.* 'Herrenhausen' is another fine form with flatter heads of a similar colour. *Origanum vulgare* 'Compactum' is a neat and obliging edging plant with a dense covering of mid-pink flowers on very short stems. For all their garden-worthiness, bees and butterflies barely recognize the superiority of these superb varieties and seem not to make any distinction or preference as they also forage for nectar amongst my inferior, mongrel seedlings which serve them just as well.

WILD WEAVERS   I often allow volunteer wildflowers or invite them in without knowing whether they will be a well-ordered guest or if they will give me a hard time. I have yet to discover whether it was wise or foolhardy to introduce tufted vetch, *Vicia cracca*, one of the loveliest, later-flowering vetches which tempts some of the meadow butterflies and moths from the meadow to the garden. The flowers combine blue, purple and pink colouring which makes them a good "mixer" as they clamber amongst plants in that colour zone. Common vetch, *Vicia sativa*, has bright pink flowers more sparsely arranged amongst the similarly fine, pinnate foliage. This vetch is earlier flowering and is a great favourite with bees. A word of caution! – the related bush vetch, *Vicia sepium*, is the vetch from hell in the garden. It is almost impossible to control or eradicate and barely redeems itself, appearance-wise, with its coarser foliage and dull flowers.

Unlike the vetches, common fumitory (*Fumaria officinalis*) has no tendrils to help it hitch a lift among its rivals in its plant community but it manages to lounge about among, or on top of, other plants. It appears in odd places where there is bare or disturbed soil so, although it was an attractive feature of the young Round Garden, fumitory has found it more difficult to keep its place as the garden planting has matured. I have found it sadly non-negotiable in this respect but I am fond of this curious little character and intend to keep trying ways to make it content. It is more than happy with conditions in my poly-tunnel so at least I have a dependable seed source. Apparently it is self-pollinating because insects ignore its ample nectar supply. I wonder what that is all about? Wild plants seldom waste resources. An extra element of mystery now creeps into the nectar garden . . .

GRASSES With all the intensity of the flowering plants I have shown, it would be easy to lose sight of the fact that the plants are mixed with grasses to remind me of my beloved meadows. There is a wealth of ornamental grasses to choose from and I have tried out many of them. Lyme grass (*Leymus arenarius*) was one of the first to be planted after I discovered it was a great favourite with Gertrude Jekyll. She must have been an intrepid lady to use a plant with a reputation for its powers to anchor its roots in sand dunes. In my early enthusiasm, I barely registered just how much regular digging would be required to thin it and restrain its threshold. I suppose Miss Jekyll had an army of gardeners to help but if the load falls on one person, it needs to land on a strong one, full of grit and determination. I waver as I try to decide if I should put myself through the same trials again, even when I see those grand, glaucous-blue blades at their most sensational in high summer. *Elymus magellanicus*, or even the finer, clumpier *Festuca mariei*, might be a better choice in a similar situation. The winter effect of any of these is modest and by the end of the year they tend to succumb to a certain amount of fungal attack, which disfigures rather than debilitates them.

WINTER GRASSES Most of my other varied grasses constitute a superb element of my Round Garden in winter. In fact, they create a whole fantastic winter scene of their own, as most of the other plants retreat into dormancy, leaving only a handful of perennials with fine, long-standing stems with seed-heads. It takes that special, low winter light and a touch of rain to reveal fully the wonder and range of the colours so often lumped together and dismissed as "buff" – even by those who claim to appreciate it. Look carefully at the leaf blades and you can see the colours of sand from the Sahara and spices from the Indies, as well as the browns, yellow-ochres and grass-greens of our British landscape in winter. I have mentioned some of the grasses but I have made no reference to one of the most exciting I know: *Miscanthus sinensis* 'Morning Light'. It seldom flowers, which means that there are no stiff flower stems to impair the way it moves in the wind, like a horse's flowing mane or a stormy sea, depending on one's mood and imagination. Its fountain of foliage has added winter colours of russet reds, which fire up and glow when diffused with winter light. Before the drama that surrounds it in winter, 'Morning Light' stands serene and gracious with its fine, silvery-green, arching leaves. It is one of the shorter miscanthus with a slightly less brutish root system than others, making it very user-friendly, especially in a smaller garden.

Pennisetum alopecuroides has strong, clumps of pleasant but plain green foliage, about 60cm (2ft) high. It begins to flower in September and its outstanding "bottle brush" flowers endure until the New Year, having run the gauntlet of silver, pinkish, greenish, and then straw, colouring. *Agrostis curvula*, or African lovegrass, is finer in details of foliage and flower and, although it is less show-stopping, I very much admire its graceful, arching form, which makes an impression for about ten months of the year. I have to thin it radically if it is to share space with other plants so I remove old plants and allow new seedlings to take their place. Grasses are wind-pollinated and although they have no nectar for insects to feed on, they are good habitat providers for hibernating insects or their overwintering larvae. The spent foliage is often tough and enduring as a nesting material for birds, reason enough to consider grasses a useful addition to the wildlife garden.

NATURAL BALANCE Like annual plants, many insects die at the end of the season and leave it to their few surviving relatives to frantically produce fresh generations as soon as the weather starts to warm up in spring. Other insects hibernate or leave a new generation to overwinter as eggs or in their larval forms. As far as gardeners are concerned, there are friends and foes among them but for the carnivorous creatures that depend on them, all are welcome fodder. I hold the belief that the broader the range of insects I encourage, the more likely the chance of achieving a happy balance where there will not be a disproportionate or overwhelming number of pest species. So far my faith has been rewarded and nowadays I seldom have to intervene and squash anything. I must confess that it took time for me to be able to say this because – remember – I began my garden on a barren site and the system only began to kick in when the garden began to mature and I had less need to interfere with the soil and the plants once they were established.

THE SEASONALITY With the range of grasses and seed-heads left intact, this garden can look most inspiring, especially on frosty mornings. The winter tracery lasts until mid-February when we gradually clear the brittle remains and "adjust the choreography" of planting in preparation for the next season of dance. Meanwhile, the birds have the opportunity to feed on seeds and insects, and field mice and voles thrive in the protection of the hitherto uncleared herbaceous aftermath. When the time comes to prepare the garden for spring and summer, we wait for dry weather before treading on the beds to cut down the remains of the winter scene and tackle the weeding, lifting, splitting and rearranging perennials. We meticulously avoid compacting the soil and damaging its structure or harming the vital soil-life.

HABITAT BOOSTERS

It is possible to buy artificial nests for bumblebees and masonry bees, and I have tried the latter with some success. In principle, bumblebees like to use holes at the base of a hedge in a shady, sheltered south-facing spot, so I have tried to oblige

them with a variety of materials, such as piles of air-bricks and half-buried, overturned, clay flower-pots to give them a well disguised and protected "front door". The rest they can do themselves if they approve my outline planning regulations. Sometimes these things work out as intended and pretty often they don't. I am often compensated and amused when a field mouse or some other creature bags the site for nesting and I am repeatedly confounded when the chosen or alternative creature makes a nest just a few feet or even inches away from my well-thought-out "eco-feature". Nature always has the last – and in this case, I suspect, the loudest – laugh!

As in all my other gardens, I tuck bundles of hollow stems of varied diameter under shrubs that I am unlikely to disturb for a while. Admittedly I find the evidence of recent occupation more often than I find the actual resident, but that is probably because some other creature has eaten it and that is what it is all about; one species feeding on another in the complex chain which God or Nature masterminded. As gardeners, we have to cross our fingers and hope it all pans out in our favour as well as for the asylum-seekers we harbour. I am convinced my various "habitat boosters" were as great an asset in the juvenile garden as they are now, when the garden is fully fledged. In the Round Garden, as in other places, there are small piles of stones, logs and hollow stems tucked away wherever they can be discreetly placed. I always save the hollow stems of herbaceous plants such as *Filipendula rubra*, *Eupatorium purpureum*, the angelicas, and motherwort. I tie them in bundles and stack them in odd places, sometimes horizontally, sometimes vertically, some placed on the earth and some laid between branches of dense shrubs, such as berberis and escalonia. Our sundial has a circular groove for holding a shallow volume of water, ideal as an insects' "bar", if I can remember to fill it regularly. Mostly they prefer to visit the pond but it is worth considering their needs and fun to watch when they respond to my offerings.

SEDUM RY *Sedum spectabile* is a plant that shares star rating with butterflies and bees and failing to mention it so far may seem like an obvious omission. In fact, this has been deliberate because I have given them special prominence in the garden. I have

A woven-willow globe takes precedence amidst a circle of *Festuca mareii*. The seats and woven-willow arbour are fully revealed at the top of the Round Garden.

clumps of sedum in the various parts of the garden borders and have watched how the insects, butterflies in particular, migrate around the circle seeking the warmest place to feed. I recently decided to give them what I hope will be their hearts' desire and concentrate this special delicacy in a sunny, almost south-facing, feature position. I have built a small flint stone bank to aid the drainage and to reduce the amount and availability of our loamy, nutrient-rich soil which has overfed them in the past; too rich a diet has caused them to grow over-lush and hefty. Hefty plants are then more prone to collapse and I believe they suffer more with fungal problems affecting the stems. Rotting stems cause disarray amongst the winter dead-heads and deep sadness for the gardener who values the winter garden as I do. I hope all these problems will be resolved and that the sedums will share the space congenially with my mongrel oreganos which I remove from places where there is less scope for allowing and appreciating their promiscuous habits.

One good reason to leave seed-heads intact in winter! Having attracted and fed an abundance of butterflies and bees in summer, the snow-capped sedums have a moment of unsurpassed winter glory as they enfold the sedumry bench.

IN CONCLUSION

There are many other good nectar plants besides the ones I have listed, including annuals such as candytuft, white alyssum, certain marigolds, mignonette, lobelia, heliotrope, single dahlias and many more. I am sure everyone can tell a different tale of the preferences that their garden population of butterflies has demonstrated. My Round Garden is constantly evolving to take on board our discoveries, both in terms of wildlife value and experimental planting compositions. It is a victory when a border turns out to be a key "crowd-pleaser" – be it a crowd of bees, butterflies, hoverflies, moths, birds or human onlookers.

In the daytime we can often hear the collective buzz and watch the gentle flutter of insects in this paradise. The most favoured plants literally "rock and roll" with wildlife. At night the moths and bats have the arena to themselves, although I confess I bear testament to very little of the shady night-life, except for the odd evenings when I have the energy to creep out and listen to the owls and the other mysterious sounds of the night; mostly I am too weary after a day's work which frequently begins at dawn.

I must admit that the Round Garden has taxed my physical and creative resources even while it has been a fantastic experience and experiment. Commonsense tells me I was over-ambitious in choosing rather too large a site for a sensible, normal person to manage as a hobby. Be that as it may, the concept could be very easily scaled down to just a few choice plants that I would – or will – take with me to the retirement home, madhouse or workhouse, depending on what the future holds!

THE
WHITE
GARDEN

With its naturalistic design and planting, this garden combines fruit, berries, perennials and grasses with ecological features to create habitats for all creatures great and small.

The maturing white border provides lessons both in the subtleties of colour and in providing for the creatures the flowers were specially selected to support.

I DOUBT IF THERE IS ANY PROBLEM persuading fellow gardeners of the joys of making their gardens attractive to birds, bees, butterflies and other positively beneficial creatures, but not all the larger mammals are ideal visitors in the garden and some can be disruptive and destructive – especially in small gardens. But who would wish to turn away a dormouse or a hedgehog?

Mice, voles and shrews can hardly be classified as "beneficial" to the garden, but a reasonably large country garden can accommodate their nibbling habits with little harm to plants once they are mature. These small mammals provide food for others in the chain; for some owls, for instance, voles are the main ingredient in their diet. It is this food chain that must be considered, and we must be especially aware of the importance of insects and invertebrates in it, both above and below the soil. Foxes will prey on almost anything they can catch, so they easily earn a living in both urban and rural gardens. Some people welcome their company though others are not amused. I find that stoats, weasels and hares are comparatively rarely found in gardens and those I have seen have been too shy to hang about for long. I expect much depends on the proximity of the garden to their more natural habitat. To be realistic, while "gardening in tune with nature" is essentially about encouraging and enjoying beneficial wildlife, it also involves negotiating with the creatures whose presence may sometimes disturb the order we seek to create.

Having been involved with the conservation of grassland for many years, I seize any opportunity I find to restore or create areas of meadow, whether they be a few yards square or several acres in size. In Britain, 98 per cent of species-rich grassland has been destroyed since the war and that devastation has resulted in lost habitat for dependent flora and fauna alike. Our natural woodland has similarly suffered, 50 per cent of it destroyed in that same period. It is almost impossible to replace such priceless habitat, and hard to imagine how gardeners can begin to make up for the irresponsible actions of our predecessors. However, we can certainly help in a small way – even with the tiniest patches of simulated woodland and meadow patches, and this was my intention in my proposed White Garden.

THE WOODLAND EDGE In the countryside some of the best wildlife habitat exists where woodland or hedgerow start to merge into open grassland (the "ecotone" in modern parlance) and the more gradual the transition, the better. On farmland this often amounts to field edges – at their most valuable when a generous margin is left between crops or pasture and the dividing or boundary hedgerow. If the hedgerow is broad and tall, with mature trees, then so much the better; there is a special bonus if there is mature, broad-leaved woodland adjoining. If such woodland is well-managed and sections of the under-storey are coppiced on a traditional ten-to-fifteen year system of rotation, the ecosystem continually improves, as the richest diversity of wildlife is supported. Wildlife can benefit from the best of all worlds where a choice of shaded places, dappled light and sunny spots offers shelter and protection for a wide range of creatures. At the same time, these assorted conditions support the growth and survival of a diversity of essential native plants on which these creatures depend. Some such individuals rely on just a single plant species for their survival. This is often the case with butterflies, such as the Hairstreaks, Fritillaries and certain Blues; no host plant in a suitable environment = no butterfly. It is as simple and sad as that.

THE SAD REALITY Unfortunately the paradigm of countryside management I have described for woodland, for example, is more or less non-existent where intensive agricultural practice maximizes the use of every square inch of ground and woods are often managed simply for the commercial growth and extraction of timber. Farm hedgerows, if they are lucky enough to survive being grubbed up to extend field acreages, are generally brutally flailed within an inch of their lives – very often at nesting time when birds are in occupation or later when they are relying on hedgerow berries for winter fodder. Field crops are grown cheek by jowl against the mutilated hedges and both are treated to a cocktail of chemicals as spray-drift often clobbers the non-targeted hedgerow species and their interdependent wildlife. So serious has the effect on the environment become that, albeit late in the day, there are government incentives to encourage farmers to care for their hedges and leave wide field margins. Sadly, the positive impact of such sustainable management seems to be fairly limited. I see little evidence of conservation – or even plain common-sense – filtering through in parts of my own county. In fact, rather the reverse is occurring where field edges are deliberately sprayed with herbicide and hedges battered and shattered during the period when birds are nesting.

THE GOOD NEWS However, although ignorance, lack of legislation, the economic climate or other reasons may prevent some landowners from caring for the environment, there are wonderful conservation organizations and also some farmers, particularly the organic growers, who manage their land in a highly sympathetic and sustainable way. Gardeners like myself can join with them through our smaller conservation efforts. We can help by very simply mimicking the desirable "ecotone principles" in our gardens. In effect we do this when we plant a combination of native and garden plants to make a smooth and progressive change from shady woodland to dappled glades to sunny open borders and then lawns. Amazingly, we can achieve this in a surprisingly small space. With two or three trees, an under-storey of a few shrubs that emerge to form the backdrop for a border of nectar-rich cottage-garden plants and herbs and a lawn, or preferably a patch of meadow close by, we have simulated the type of habitat that will provide a safe haven for a wealth of creatures which will, in turn, benefit our gardens. Threading in a few British native plants as well as choosing trees and shrubs with fruits and berries adds to the wealth of our bequest. If sympathetically – and preferably organically – managed, our garden habit can be a jewel for at least some of the wildlife displaced from the ever more hostile countryside.

THE DESIGN BRIEF

The white wilderness I had in mind was to be the last part of our two acres of garden to be designed and cultivated. My aim was to use this area to mimic the woodland edge (or ecotone) habitat and also to create a half-acre wildflower meadow. After the constraints that are an inevitable part of planting and managing our Round Garden with its formal, geometric pattern, I felt the urge to make our final garden space one of comparative freedom and with a greater sense of open space and interrelationship with our surroundings. However, the White Garden was barely a twinkle in the eye until 1990 when we planted the first trees to establish a framework for a garden in which we could extend our interest in combining garden planting with native plants and grasses. We wanted this garden to appear to melt imperceptibly into the background as it merged with our hedgerows, meadow, smallholding, neighbouring farmland and the wider landscape beyond. It was part of our original aim to make sure our garden project would blend unobtrusively, rather than intrude conspicuously, on the bucolic charm of the Blackmore Vale countryside. Here, on the higher point of our land we could view the widened horizons with views extending to Dorset's famous Bulbarrow Hill.

To help strengthen the defences against potential marauders, one of the very first things we did in 1987 was to widen the northern boundary of the small-holding by making a small band of woodland, with additional oaks, ash and beech. Although commonly found in the countryside, beech is not a British native tree. It supports only a few insects but the masts are valuable food for tits, chaffinches, bramblings, greater-spotted woodpeckers and nuthatches. We introduced three poplars: the black poplar (*Populus nigra*) would hopefully become home to the Poplar Hawk-moth; the grey poplar (*Populus x canescens*) was included to look beautiful and match others in our local landscape, and *Populus balsamifera* would waft its most delicious, balmy scent downwind across our land.

We underplanted the new trees with hazel and field maple. Near the front woodland edge we added cherry plum, wild crab apple, wild pear and damson, which all have thorny stems, and wild cherry with guelder rose and wayfaring tree in between with wild honeysuckle intertwining among them. The hazel would be coppiced about every 12 years to let light in and regenerate the growth of plants on the woodland floor. Once the light levels had begun to shade out the nettles, we would introduce the local English bluebells we had been given by our neighbour and which we were multiplying in nursery beds.

This part of our land is at the edge of the smallholding and has a substantial bank and ditch, which is the territory of badgers. We hoped they would be content to stay there rather than disturb our garden and, in fact, we have seen very little of them in recent years, the only evidence being the removal of ground-based wasp nests. It is strange, considering their diet can include about 250 worms per night, that we see so few signs of disruption from their foraging. With our extra scrub planting, we crossed our fingers and hoped to increase the chances that dormice would travel along the hedgerows of the neighbouring farmland and connect to this little oasis of coppiced woodland habitat. Foxes come and go, and for two consecutive years we had a resident vixen who reared an enchanting litter of cubs in the White Garden. Rabbits are more permanent inhabitants and, with some extra protection for young plants, we managed an acceptable level of co-existence while our whippets were young and agile hunters and before our cats became geriatric and disinclined to stalk them.

GARDEN STYLE I decided on an informal style – a far cry from the more traditional concept of the "white garden". There are many famous formal white gardens, none better than Vita Sackville-West's beautiful garden at Sissinghurst. At Sticky Wicket our starting point was quite different. My planting would not be so strictly design-led nor correspondingly subject to the constraints of formality. I wanted to encourage spontaneity, interfere as little as possible and to have a steady programme of development that would eventually allow more of a "white wilderness" to evolve as the garden matured. I wanted a "garden for all seasons" that would generate yet more wildlife habitat and be robust enough to support some of the larger, furry creatures; a garden in which I could constantly learn from the experience of trying to sketch a fine line between a reasonably acceptable level of order and escalating chaos. In order for the garden to bring joy to humans as well as providing a haven for some larger wildlife, there would be an inevitable conflict of interest and a need for compromise. In short, I wanted to discover the parameters of garden anarchy! It is disingenuous to suggest that managing wild gardens is an effortless task, but I was convinced it would be far less stressful than trying to maintain the necessary order required by conventional borders.

THE PLAN My plan was a very simple cross-banding of approximately 65m- (70yd-) long grass paths leading to the five essential elements: the hen-run gate by "Africa House" – a sort of gazebo for hens; our shepherd's hut, which acts as a summerhouse; the two entrances to the meadow and the one that secretly disappears into the utility area, compost and recycling bay – the "engine room" of our organic garden management scheme. The grass paths would vary in width, creating an imperceptible false perspective at some points and facilitating extra open space, for a picnic or other such gathering.

SHELTER, SCREENING, SAFETY AND SCALE These were the first things to consider. I wanted the site to be protected from the elements and there were less lovely parts of the smallholding which I needed to screen. I had to take care to do this without blotting out any of the cherished views across the countryside. Peter and I also had to make sure the hen-run was safe from foxes and the garden safe from horses and goats, which meant that electric fencing would be necessary to reinforce the security. For my overall concept to work, I tried to judge the scale of the allotted areas and the perspective of design. I wanted to make the garden seem as extensive and yet as mysterious as possible and, at the same time, I had to decide where and how to make the gentle transition from shady wooded places to sunny open borders or grassland.

DOMESTIC WHITE ANIMALS   It may be said that I forced the design issue somewhat unduly by choosing white animals as "living statuary". I admit that doves (and their white dovecote) were certainly intended to be a feature here. They may interbreed to gain a few odd colours but they are genetically principally white, so that was acceptable. But there are also white animals in the pens and paddocks that are within or close to the garden. Some of our bantams have dodgy origins and come in assorted colours, but our first choice was to acquire and help conserve an old English breed – the Light Sussex – which happens to be white with black markings. The snow geese were rescued from an uncertain fate and the breed is nearly always white, so the choice was made for us there. Only one of our four ducks is white but she is certainly the most conspicuous. Saanan goats – also white – are good milkers, lovely characters and I have kept them for years. The "white" horses? Well, I have always favoured grey horses and again my association with them goes back many years "pre-Wicket". My case rests on sentimental grounds. I must admit, I do get a great thrill out of seeing my white pets in close proximity to the white planting! There is also the fact that both the white plants and animals contribute towards the gentle ambience of morning mistiness and the contrastingly eerie evening atmosphere which I wanted to intensify. At least I resisted the notion of having a white peacock; that would have been one pretentious step too far for a wildlife gardener and smallholder!

PLANTING BRIEF

My brief, as always, was to choose hardy stalwarts to provide pollen, nectar, seeds, fruit, berries, nuts or form protective wildlife habitat. The habitat element was intended to be a particular strength in this garden. As ever, I would arrange all my plants so as to draw attention to their natural beauty but here there was to be a somewhat wilder approach compared to the planting associations in the more disciplined domain of the previous gardens. I wanted to make a rambling and romantic garden where wafting fragrances filled the air and where there was a strong winter effect from coloured stems or from those that were otherwise effective in their winter nakedness. I decided to up the stakes on the conservation of wildflowers and mingle a plethora of them among their only slightly more exotic bedfellows. In this wilder garden I wanted to experiment with growing grasses, both ornamental and native, in a way that would take "naturalism" to a new level. Both grasses and wildflowers in the borders, mixed with garden plants, would prepare a visually gentle passage to those in a nearby garden meadow or "flowery mead", as I ambitiously perceived it would one day be.

My selected plants would hopefully cater for insects, birds, foxes, field mice and any other creatures that might care to live among them. I admit to hoping the badgers would continue to stay in their nearby hedgerows away from the garden and that deer would not wander in, but in the event of their occupation, the matured garden would hopefully be robust enough for all to co-exist. Rabbits are an inevitable part of country life and I braced myself for negotiation and probably a little conflict in this wilder setting. This garden was for "all creatures great and small" and that involved a different level of tolerance from previous gardens, where rabbits had been discouraged by our dogs or held at bay by rabbit-proof fencing. I am not opposed to the idea of shooting the odd rabbit for the pot, but in principle I didn't want to have to fight over this garden or to assert undue control over it. I wanted to nudge things along in a pragmatic way, as I believed this was how it should be with a "wilderness" garden.

WHITE-FLOWERED GARDEN PLANTS   In selecting my white-flowered trees and shrubs, I was delighted to discover what an extensive and pertinent range was available to me. Most fruit-, hip- and berry-bearing plants have white flowers and many have the bonus of autumn colour, so we would be able to see an exciting colour transformation happening as summer faded and both foliage and berries would begin to light up the landscape. To add to this and for winter delight I could include trees and shrubs with coloured, patterned or spectacularly thorny stems. As usual, I yearned for a sequence of scented plants at all points of the garden. The criteria were very easy to meet. There is a preponderance of white forms of garden plants, including deliciously scented ones. There are dozens of white wildflowers which can be pleasingly integrated with the relaxed style of planting I favour, so I was spoiled for choice. I kept strictly on course and resisted any temptation to stray into selecting exotic or unusual plants for the sake of "plantsmanship" or, heaven forbid, "plant one-up-manship."

I had a lot to learn about the vagaries of the plant colour we loosely term "white". I began to divide my plants into those with hints and undertones of pink, cream, yellow, green or blue and also the rather understated russet and bronze tints. The subtle colour influences can be induced by the colour of the surrounding foliage of the plant, its bracts, stem buds, stamen, central eye or the underside or veins of petals. I discovered that very few plants are actually pure white but some are whiter than others, and can make the tinted ones look rather dirty if the placing is ill-considered. Naturally these observations went hand-in-glove with discovering which of my selected wildlife-friendly plants were to be most valuable and also which ones would be sturdy and reasonably rabbit-resistant.

CONSTRUCTION

For a harmonious coexistence between gardener and garden wildlife, it helps if parameters are set either physically or at least in one's mind. I did not want to show zero tolerance to any creature but I had misgivings about one or two of those in the vicinity and I needed to set out my strategy with regard to creating exclusion zones.

WILDLIFE DEFENCES Fortunately we have no problem with deer and therefore no need to try to fence them out. Badgers seldom bother us but I know they can be a bit disruptive, especially if their chosen route is made in any way inaccessible to them. Where badgers are in residence I think it wise to give in and design the garden around their regularly used tracks because they become extremely belligerent when obstacles are placed to exclude or divert them. Peter and I have mixed feelings about foxes because, although we love to see them, and they help thin the rabbit population, there is always the terrible fear they will penetrate our defences and massacre our poultry and waterfowl. To separate fox from fowl, we constructed a 1.8m (6ft) fence with a strand of electric wire top and bottom. The bottom one was just 15cm (6in) away from the base of the wire netting and this netting was also laid along the ground for 30cm (12in) to further thwart the attempts of any animal trying to dig its way in.

A similar fence, but just 1m (3¼ft) high would have been necessary if we had been determined to exclude rabbits from all of the gardens, but the costs involved and the amount of maintenance required meant that this was not even a consideration. To include the White Garden we would have needed to cater for the comings and goings of badgers, including special gates so that they had access and, in my experience, this never fails to rub them up the wrong way and incites sabotage.

MOLES, MICE, VOLES AND EGG-STEALERS Of course, moles cannot be fenced out and, in my opinion, life is too short to devote the time required to try to trap them or to play games with the windmills, upturned bottles, garlic or moth-balls intended to repel them or drive them at least as far as the property next door! I just spread the big heaps of mole-hill soil where they pop up, or use some for potting compost, and I try to comfort myself that they help keep the ground aerated in winter. Admittedly I get more than a little "aerated" myself when I consider the vast number of earthworms they devour. Worms are most efficient and valuable conditioners of soil and we need their input. When mole damage is just too rife and conspicuous, Peter, blessed with the patience of Jove and the persistence of a saint, would sometimes stalk and shoot them when he saw fresh soil erupting as they worked their four-hourly tunnelling shifts. That solved the problem for just the amount of time it takes for another mole to take the place of the dead one. Naturally we would rather put up with them than even for one moment consider poisoning or gassing them. Goodness knows how many other creatures could become the innocent victims of such draconian measures.

Shrews, mice and voles may annoyingly nibble a few plants and bulbs but they are food for owls and other predators. I catch only a fleeting glimpse of them, but I often find rather enchanting little nests in both likely and improbable places. Field mice include worms and snails in their diet so, as with so many of these mammals, there are pros and cons for the gardener to evaluate, who sometimes eradicates friends along with foes. Hedgehogs consume slugs, caterpillars and also insect larvae, some of which are pests to the gardener and some of which, such as beetles, are an asset. They also eat birds' eggs and chicks and, I am told, will even kill snakes. On balance, hedgehogs are a friend to the gardener and are fascinating animals to have visit our gardens, where they can at least be temporarily safe from the hazards of the traffic that accounts for a large percentage of their high mortality rate.

Stoats, weasels and grey squirrels are fascinating to watch but they also steal birds' eggs. Stoats compensate for their destructiveness by catching rats, which definitely need to be controlled, and rabbits, which become more manageable when their numbers are reduced. Owls and hawks will, in turn, take the stoats as well as weasels, which are Britain's smallest carnivores and half the size of a stoat. Weasels prey on mice, voles, and occasionally even a rabbit. The harsh reality of nature's system has to be faced and it can be tough.

Grey squirrels, cute-looking as they may be, are the most persistent, up-front and provocative in their hedgerow-raiding activities. They also vandalize trees with their bark-stripping habits. Being aliens to this country they have no natural predators to balance the numbers. All these predatory mammals are a law unto themselves and there is no practical physical barrier to prohibit them so we just have to take them on board if they choose to drop in or become resident. The only way nesting song-birds can avoid such predators is by finding a dense, well-camouflaged site, which is difficult for invaders to penetrate.

There are mixed feelings among ecologists regarding interference with other predators, such as crows, magpies and sparrowhawks. The latter are protected but the former two can be controlled with a gun or, in the case of magpies (if their numbers are excessive), using live bait, in the form of one of their own kind, to lure them into a Larsen trap. After witnessing a lethal raid on a precious thrush's nest, I was not unduly disturbed when our neighbour culled either the culprit or at least one or two of his relations.

PROGRAMME OF WORK Having faced the fact that trials and tribulations exist with certain wildlife, I will now re-focus on the pleasures of attracting more benevolent creatures desperately needing the protection and food our gardens can offer.

I was in no hurry to complete this garden so it was planted in three logical phases, starting in 1990. We set out the design by mowing the intended pattern in the long grass of what was still rough pasture, Peter swiftly wielding the machinery once I had set out the simple design in the morning dew. We very carefully positioned and then planted the considered framework of trees, including cherries, crab apples, rowans and hawthorns. I had in mind a small fruit forest where the bounty would be shared by all the inhabitants, human or otherwise. We also planted two groups of nine birches to form small, wooded places dissected by bark paths.

The trees were generously mulched with two or three inches of wood peelings, securely protected with spiral guards against rabbit damage and further protected by a wide surround of rails and stock wire. This defence would keep them safe while both our goats and horses continued to graze the remaining grassland during the two years we would allow for the trees to begin to mature. I prefer to plant small trees and wait for them to grow healthily, at their own pace, rather than planting large trees, which can struggle rather feebly unless mollycoddled and consistently irrigated. I used the interim time to propagate some of the shrubs and most of the perennials I had in mind for future planting.

SPRING 1992 Once the trees were well established, our stock were permanently banished from the site as we set out the rest of the design once more – this time for real. In spring we began the process of double-digging and manuring the borders and then dealing with the first flushes of weed growth, allowing a whole summer to pass before we began to plant into the cleaned and conditioned soil. As ever, our border preparations were thorough and time allowed for repeated applications of garden compost and manure. We were soon to be handsomely repaid by the rapid and healthy growth of the plants and the minimal need to water them.

Where grassy paths were intended, we persuaded the existing pasture turf to be a little more lawn-like simply by a summer regime of occasional light rolling and regular mowing. We also designated a 60 by 6m (70 by 7yd) area of long grass to be converted from rough pasture to "garden meadow", where wildflowers and selected garden plants would hopefully grow side by side. This garden meadow

would form the fringe between the White Garden and the "pukka" wildflower hay-meadow we hoped one day to create still further beyond.

AUTUMN 1992 — THE SHRUB PLANTING   I planted an under-storey of shrubs beneath some of the trees and a framework of shrubs for the mixed borders in the more open spaces nearby. Once more, the new plants were treated to a thick mulch of pulverized bark from our local timber growers. But how were the rabbits to know the plants had not been provided to cater for their appetites? At first all the plants had to be individually protected with wire or plastic mesh surrounds; we used beige-coloured clematis netting, which looked reasonably unobtrusive. Rabbits seem particularly attracted to new plants set into bare ground. When the novelty had worn off and the plants were well grown, the protection was removed while we apprehensively watched and waited to appraise their activities. Meanwhile, we erected the white wooden dovecote; we started with just two pairs of doves and now have around thirty.

SPRING 1993 — THE HERBACEOUS PLANTS   I began to introduce some of the herbaceous plants, including ornamental grasses which would complement the tints and tones of the flowers and foliage of the shrubs, and help to provide ground cover and, of course, sustenance for wildlife. Once more we had to try and outwit the rabbits or simply give up attempting to grow the plants they found most irresistible. They have a frustrating and unreasonable way of changing their preferences just when you think you have the measure of their appetites.

The struggle to persuade wildflowers to grow in the over-fertile soil of the garden meadow led me to an experiment; I tried killing off the existing turf by smothering it with plastic before setting some small plants and re-seeding. Unfortunately, this proved a hopeless idea as the same grasses and weeds returned with a vengeance. I had to keep digging them out, along with their clods of topsoil, until the nutrient level started to abate; it took several years before I could coax the wildflowers to establish themselves. I also sowed yellow rattle, a semi-parasitic native plant, to help

We mowed wide grassy paths to form the template of the very simple design needed to accommodate domestic fowl and doves. Having previously planted about forty strategically sited trees, we began to prepare and plant the borders around them.

suppress the growth of the grasses. Gradually I began to naturalize a few suitably competitive garden plants, such as hardy geraniums, and after several years, my romantic notion of the "flowery mead" began to take shape.

AUTUMN 1993 — THE SHEPHERD'S HUT AND SHEEPFOLD   By now we had foxes breeding in the hedgerows and regularly visiting the garden with their cubs. We needed a sheltered place to observe our charming guests and Peter resolved to find a suitable building. He took himself off to the Great Dorset Steam Fair, struck a deal with a colourful local character, and returned the proud owner of a shepherd's hut; the perfect choice of shelter for our location and the general ambience of this outer garden. (Shepherds originally lived in these mobile, corrugated iron shacks at lambing time; the huts would be towed to the distant fields or downs so the shepherd could be on hand to attend his flock.) "Haycombe One" – as ours was called – was towed into place at the furthest end of the garden, adjoining the meadow.

Our hut, honourably retired from lambing service, is now both a wildlife hide and a resting spot, and a place to display information about wildlife gardening for our visitors. In winter it provides exactly the right temperature for butterflies and

lacewings to hibernate. We have recently watched a young stoat playfully popping in and out of the undercarriage; foxes, too, sometimes shelter between the huge metal wheels in the 60cm- (2ft-) deep space below the hut. While it may be perfect heaven for the stoats and foxes, it is highly disconcerting for our domestic fowl in the run immediately beside the wildlife squat. A line of electric fence has so far dissuaded the foxes from carrying out a deadly raid. We play with fire when we try to divide such tempting prey from their natural predators. Fortunately, our hens roost high in our alder trees and the more vulnerable ducks and geese have a reasonably large pond for refuge in the event of attack.

The design for our "sheepfold" was inspired by one of Gordon Beningfield's paintings. Gordon was an exceptional artist and conservationist who loved Dorset and often chose shepherd's huts as a subject for his work. One such painting portrays a straw-bale sheepfold enclosure next to a hut. I re-interpreted this with a willow-woven "sheepfold" beside our hut and within the nearby, recently planted birch copse. We used ash poles for stakes and then wove long wands of willow in a diagonal pattern to complete a semi-circular shape. There is a break in the structure to allow access and make a tempting entrance to the meadow. The sheepfold is underplanted with a combination of white woodland plants and grasses, which compliment the white bark of the birches.

AUTUMN 1997 After five years of trying to achieve my heart's desire with the strip of garden meadow, I finally grasped the problem of the extreme fertility of our soil. The battle to suppress the vigorous grasses and creeping buttercup proved much harder than the removal of the odd dock or nettle – also indicating the fertile nature of my rich loam. After several experiments, I realized a more radical approach would be required if Peter and I were to tackle the next half-acre area we had in mind.

In September 1997 we made a dramatic departure from our rule of hand-digging only and excavated the site with a JCB. We removed hundreds of tons of topsoil to reveal an infertile subsoil much more conducive to growing wildflowers. With the removal of the turf went the layer of Yorkshire fog grass, creeping buttercup and

The "woodland-edge" habitat (to the left) and the garden-meadow grassland habitat (to the right) flank the path to the former shepherd's hut that serves as a wildlife hide and information centre for our visitors.

white clover, which had hampered our previous grassland restoration programmes.

This huge ecological disruption would never have been contemplated had we not been utterly convinced that the ends would justify the means. The combination of the flower-rich grassland with the nearby woodland, hedgerow and garden habitat would offer extended opportunities for an even wider range of wildlife to flourish. A friend and conservationist had advised me and offered some locally sourced wildflower seed from his own project nearby, so that with this priceless gift we would also be able to make a significant contribution to the conservation of the grassland flora (and the associated wildlife) of our part of Dorset. (I have described this venture in my first book, *Making Wildflower Meadows*.)

Not wanting to part with the displaced topsoil, we built a feature known as "Mount Wicket" with the spoil from the excavation. This upwardly extended the grazing area for our goats, which had been systematically robbed as the garden encroached on their territory. This turned out to be just the place for voles to live and (unfortunately for them) to become, in their turn, the favoured food for the owls we hear all around our property. The rich soil is conducive to the growth of a luxuriant crop of nettles and with a little extra management from us – cutting about three-quarters of them down in June to regenerate fresh growth – they provide a perfect and well-used maternity unit for caterpillars of the Peacock, Red Admiral and Small Tortoiseshell butterflies.

PLANTING

To make the flowering period of the garden as extensive as possible, we celebrate the arrival of the New Year with hellebores and carpets of bulbs in the borders, the birch woodland and especially in the garden meadow. One of the most stimulating sounds is that of the early bumblebees trying to squeeze themselves into the flowers of *Helleborus foetidus*. When I hear that buzz and see snowdrops and narcissi forging their way upwards, I know the earth is stirring and it is time for me to increase my gardening activities. I keep the floral momentum going with trees, shrubs and herbaceous plants that flower in a measured sequence until late October with late-flowering asters and Japanese anemones, together with late-flowering shrubs such as *Clerodendron trichotomum var. fargesii*. Thus there continues a succession of hips and berries for more or less twelve months of the year.

SHARING THE PRODUCE   The 17th-century essayist, Joseph Addison, wrote, "I value my garden more for birds than for cherries and very frankly give them fruit for their song". What fine sentiments! I keep repeating this when a consistently charitable attitude is needed at raspberry, gooseberry and black-, red- and white-currant time, when I would be grateful if they would sometimes share the pickings with me just a little more charitably. To be fair, they do leave me a very reasonable share of delicious, raspberry-like Japanese wineberries. Do I imagine it or are white-fruited alpine strawberries even more flavoursome than the red ones? They seem to taste as if they have had the cream added and the birds have gradually learnt to recognize them for the delicacy they are. I could possibly build a fruit cage to protect my portion of the fruit but it would have to be 100 per cent sound and solid to eliminate any risk of having birds trapped in floppy netting. I would rather take my chance and accept a more meagre ration than be responsible for such a catastrophe. I can hardly complain since I introduced most of the plants with the deliberate intention of providing for wildlife; my reward is the endless hours of pleasure in watching and hearing the results. And what a result we are having!

TREES WITH FRUIT OR BERRIES   The wild cherry (Prunus avium) is ideal in a wild garden setting, as its large leaves produce a shaded canopy. It often suckers rather annoyingly and is a greedy beast for a small garden, but I was fortunate to be able to allow my group of three plenty of room to spread and form a mini-wooded environment for flora and fauna. The blackbirds cherry-pick before the fruits are ripe enough for us to eat so we seldom even notice their rapid disappearance. My most popular bird-attracting garden tree is Malus hupehensis with its bright red, cherry-sized crab-apples. In spring its clusters of white, almond-scented blossoms are visited by hundreds of eager honey-bees. The bees are just as keen on the hawthorn (Crataegus crus-galli) and there is a very audible buzz from the direction of my trio which stand at the edge of the garden meadow. Like the malus, it has stunning autumn colour, is simply covered in berries and has a very fine winter shape with the substantial thorns that give it its name. The rowan (Sorbus aucuparia) is a comparatively slender, white-flowered tree and its large clusters of orange berries are usually eaten almost as soon as they ripen in August. I think rowans are happiest in drier conditions but mine survives well enough to contribute to the "fruits of the forest" and stimulate my curiosity in the folk-law aspect of this magical tree. The wild pear (Pyrus communis) has fruits with too sharp and dry a flavour for our palates, but they are totally acceptable to the wasps and birds that are not so discerning. The medlar (*Mespilus germanica*) is a small, white-flowered tree with a unique character; well-spaced, spreading branches with strange-looking fruits with olive-brown russeted skin and a peculiar "orifice" at the base. Who eats it? Well, once it is thoroughly over-ripe – or "bletted" – I make a sort of jam which has been pronounced "unusual" by polite friends; I think the birds eventually eat the remainder if other, more favoured fruits have been devoured by mid-winter.

MULTI-ATTRIBUTED SHRUBS Among the shrubs, the shiny black berries of both *Amelanchier lamarckii* and *Aronia melanocarpa* are usually amongst the first to be eaten and then the autumn foliage of both plants is exceptional. *Amelanchier*, or June berry commonly, has berries which are a special treat for thrushes and blackcaps – two of our favourite songbirds. The evergreen *Sarcococca confusa* has red/black berries that

they don't seem to be a particular magnet for birds. I grow it more for the heady delights of its wafting winter perfume. On the other hand, birds very soon devour the white berries of *Cornus alba* 'Elegantissima'. This plant is certainly a "good act" with its green-and-white splashed leaves, white berries and its vibrant, bright red winter stem. It is more than happy to grow in a soggy part of the border where many other plants would struggle to survive the wet winters.

With other eye-catching winter stems in mind, I grow two forms of rubus, which prefer drier ground and need plenty of space to spread. Most rubus are hard to confine and although well suited to a wilderness garden, they could be troublesome in a more genteel and confined space. I am very taken with the cool, purple-tinged, white-grey bloom of the winter stem of *Rubus biflorus*. It can look agreeably weird in a certain light. I slow down its relentless advance by planting it in grass and then tackling the ensuing chaos in late winter, when I am almost certain to find the remains of a nest towards the centre of the clump. *Rubus phoenicolasius*, the Japanese wine-berry I mentioned earlier, has contrastingly warm-looking stems with a multitude of tiny red bristles, giving the younger stems an astonishing, incandescent appearance when backlit by winter sunlight.

The extraordinary raspberry-pink and orange fruits of the spindles are four-lobed seed capsules. They are not an immediate pull for wildlife but, although they are inconspicuous in summer, they certainly declare their identity and become human crowd-pleasers in autumn. In fact, all who encounter *Euonymus planipes* are simply bowled over by the large, flamboyant berries and the fiery autumn foliage. Winged spindle (*Euonymus alatus*) competes for attention with its vivid autumn foliage, but has only small purple and red fruits. Particularly pronounced, corky, winged stems are an additional characteristic of this plant and of its rather attractive compact form, *Euonymus alatus* 'Compactus'. *Euonymus europaeus* 'Red Cascade' has smart green stems, the foliage is slightly less spectacular colour-wise and it has smaller fruits than E. *planipes* but has a very pleasing shape (as its name suggests) and I find it easier to integrate into the mixed borders. The wild spindle (*Euonymus europaeus*) adds extra colour to a rich hedgerow collection of red, white and blue-black hips and berries.

A range of hips and berries and autumn foliage of shrubs give the White Garden a dramatic seasonal colour transformation. As summer fades, *Euonymus alatus* 'Compactus' and the even more flamboyant E. *planipes* have their moment of glory.

Of my 16 varieties of cotoneaster in the whole two-acre garden, most are red berried and all have flowers that are very sought after by bees. Forms of *Cotoneaster horizontalis* have berries that are the early favourite with the birds and others seem to be eaten in a fairly predictable order through the season. *Cotoneaster x watereri* 'John Waterer', at the other extreme, is the tallest shrub (or small tree) and the mass of berries are usually left until after Christmas. *Cotoneaster bullatus* arrived as a self-seeded volunteer and I welcome it for its blood-red berries and harlequin autumn colour.

The grey-leaved sea buckthorn, *Hippophae rhamnoides*, is well laden with succulent orange berries and has the added benefit of being armed with substantial thorns. Most years see the berries stripped by visiting fieldfares or redwings on their migratory passage. The same raiders often return for the C. x w. 'John Waterer' berries. Lovely as it is to see the migrants, I feel very sorry for the resident blackbirds which seem to have jealously guarded the plant for many weeks.

THICKETS AND THORNY PLANTS FOR HABITAT   A wildlife wilderness needs thickets to give cover and, design-wise, to add to the sense that all is not quite revealed, accessible or entirely controlled. I try to enter the mind of a hedgehog, slow-worm, bird or a mouse and think what, for them, would represent a safe, protected environment. For instance, tuckering down or nesting in – or beneath – a tangle of unclipped evergreen privet, a thorny pyracantha or a hawthorn hedge bottom would seem like a snug, safe and private little kingdom.

Tangled thickets are also excellent warm roosts for birds in winter and offer secret hideouts to nest in spring. *Stephanandra incisa* is one such thicket-forming shrub. Its stems grow arm over arm, forming a very dense, medium-height shrub with an arching habitat. It has clusters of tiny, rather insignificant white flowers and crinkly leaves that turn into a rather sophisticated mosaic of autumn colour. As the leaves fall, its shiny, tan, zigzag stems are revealed and the skeleton becomes a major player in the winter garden. Its relative, *Stephanandra tanakae*, has similar flowers, fine golden autumn colour and notable impressive stems in winter, but its form is far less complex and it is taller and more open-branched. Both varieties do well in sun or

From shady woodland and thorny thickets to open meadowland this garden is intended as a sanctuary for all creatures great and small. Domestic fowl are provided with their own featured accommodation!

shade. Seldom do plants make a more congested mass of stems than *Viburnum opulus* 'Compactum' but all this activity seems to be at the expense of berry-production.

Only a foolhardy marauder or one with a death wish would meddle with my large semi-arching tangle of barberry (*Berberis vulgaris*) so I expect any pair of birds that reserve that pitch for nesting are among the safest of families in the garden. This wild plant has useful herbal attributes, including edible berries which birds ignore. Now that it has an irretrievable bramble interwoven with it, life is even safer for wildlife yet rather testing for a gardener. *Rosa grandiflora* adds to the affray; it is a suckering species rose, which also has a great ability to harbour weeds in its root system. I forgive all as I tussle with its nettles because it is so beautiful and so healthy, and such little trouble otherwise. It has quite large, single, creamy-white flowers with the conspicuous stamens that I love to see in a rose. By forging its way among other shrubs, it gives them the benefit of added thorny security while gifting yet other plants the apparent addition of unfamiliar blooms; a rather amusing spoof.

EVERGREENS Our native holly (*Ilex aquifolium*) and butcher's broom (*Ruscus aculeatus*) both bear red berries and have prickly leaves so they are useful to wildlife for both food and protected habitat. Wild privet (*Ligustrum vulgare*) has no prickly defense but has black berries and is the nectar and food plant for the impressive Privet Hawk-moth. I include these three plants at the edge of both my small woodlands and in the boundary hedge. Conifers do not provide much food for birds but they are certainly used as snug places to roost. I am not keen on any of the conspicuously shaped conifers but I do grow a few Scots pines (*Pinus sylvestris*) for a couple of reasons. Firstly, there are mature pines growing in my neighbour's garden and I wanted to make the connection with the local landscape. Secondly, they are very attractive to many tits, including coal tits and long-tailed tits, and to the tiniest of our native birds – the goldcrest.

Of the non-native evergreens, laurel (*Prunus laurocerasus*) and bay laurel (*Laurus nobilis*) can provide useful nesting habitat, have white flowers that are attractive to bees and bear shiny black berries, but the plants are just too lumbering and solid-looking for my liking. I can tolerate the darker green Portuguese laurel (*Prunus lusitanica*) or *Prunus laurocerasus* 'Otto Luyken' which has a more forgiving form and serves wildlife equally well. I leave room for thickets of evergreens such as shrubby loniceras, just as I have in the Bird Garden, and underplant one or two of my trees with box (*Buxus sempervirens*) that is allowed to grow in its natural form. Prickly pyracanthas boost both the armoured, evergreen framework and the pollen, nectar and berry supply. *Pyracantha atalantioides* is my favourite because both the flowers and the orange berries have a delicacy and subtlety lacking in some of the modern varieties.

ROSEHIPS I grow several white-flowered climbing roses that are prickly and hip-bearing. Among these, 'Bobbie James' is one of the most beautiful and vigorous and yet it is 'Seagull', now having scaled a Scots pine, that receives the most admiration for both flower, foliage and prettier hips. 'Wickwar', with sea-green foliage and the most orange of all the hips, has reached high into the cherry trees and cascades downwards. The shrubby *Rosa sericea* subsp. *omiensis* f. *pteracantha* has unusual flagon-shaped hips and looks totally fierce and unapproachable with its huge, blood-red, young thorns and its gnarly old brown ones. In fact its bark is worse than its bite when it comes to the pruning, which is necessary to encourage the blood-red thorns. It is another white-flowered, hip-producing shrub rose, *Rosa* 'Pleine de

Grace', that is the most ferocious in this respect. I take revenge and chop her exceedingly vicious prunings into 60-90cm (2-3ft) lengths to make an impenetrable lid to one of my eco-heaps. (And then I go indoors and treat my wounds!) All these aggressive plants help confound and repel the enemies of nesting birds. Thorny habitat provides a considerable safety factor when it comes to nesting. What a bonus if those plants can offer food as well as protection and, at the same time, dazzle us with their beauty and fill the air with perfume.

SCENTED PLANTS   Among my scented shrubs, the fragrance of philadelphus exemplifies to me all that is magical about the summer garden. I have three favourites: *Philadelphus microphyllus*, which has delicate, slightly arching stems with small leaves and masses of sweetly scented flowers and P. 'Beauclerk', which is contrastingly bold structure-wise and has impressive, open, back–to-back flowers with a sumptuous scent. My third choice is the more unusual *Philadelphus delavayi* which falls somewhere between the two in its form and has a purple blotch at the centre of its pretty, richly fragrant flowers. I am not usually impressed with the over-sized, waxy flowers of magnolias, especially after the inevitable frost damage which gives them that unattractive brown edge. But *Magnolia wilsonii* is in a different league. Its pure white, waxy, pendulous flowers hang gracefully, revealing prominent red stamens and drawing one to sample the heavenly citrus fragrance. They flower later in the year, avoiding any treacherous cold spring snaps.

Choisya ternata is always good value for its ability to produce a long succession of orange-blossom-like, scented flowers and to have reliable evergreen and aromatic foliage. *Clerodendrum trichotomum* var. *fargesii* also has scented flowers and aromatic foliage but it is a bitter-sweet combination because, while the August-flowering blooms are pleasantly fragrant, the faintly purple-tinged leaves, when touched or bruised, have an abrasive bitterness. I rather admire it for this quirk and for its fascinating and totally unique berries, which are surrounded by red calyces and vary from sage green to jade blue. I cannot claim that these shrubs are particularly valuable to wildlife but they make the wildlife gardener very happy in her work!

Among my fragrant herbaceous plants, *Phlox paniculata* 'White Admiral' and *Lupinus* 'Noble Maiden' make amends to nectar-seeking insects. The lupin is a great attraction for bumblebees and its white flowers, which are greenish-yellow in bud, have a strong, evocative, peppery scent. Butterflies are among other insects that visit the pure white scented flowers of the phlox, which begins to flower as the lupin fades. In spring, sweet white violets are there for bees and for certain butterfly larvae – should I eventually be so lucky as to have fritillaries breeding at Sticky Wicket.

OTHER HERBACEOUS PLANTS   Other outstanding plants for nectar include *Echinacea purpurea* 'White Swan', *Sedum spectabile* 'Iceberg' and, to a lesser extent *Lysimachia clethroides*. I am surprised that butterflies also nectar on *Anaphalis margaritacea*; it is so dry looking with nothing oozing to be seen. One of my favourite plants is the elegant *Veronicastrum virginicum* f. *alba*, a classy plant with tall, slender spires that attract a buzz of bees. The seed-heads last well and the stately effect goes on for months into winter. The silvery, globe-shaped flowers of *Echinops* 'Nivalis' are another draw for bumblebees and the seed-heads also last for several weeks. *Chamerion* (syn. *Epilobium*) *angustifolium* 'Album' is a striking form of our native rosebay willowherb. If all goes to plan, it will hopefully support the larvae of the spectacular Elephant

Hawkmoth. Although it rarely sets seed, this willowherb spreads its root system just as fast as its pink relation so it needs to be positioned where it can be allowed space to do so. Admired by humans more than wildlife, the delicately pink-tinged *Gillenia trifoliata* has such a mass covering of flowers that it is often mistaken for a shrub. Of the lower-growing, ground-covering plants, *Pulmonaria* 'Sissinghurst White' is one of the first to flower in readiness for the early bees that eagerly congregate round its snow-white flowers. There are several white species and varieties of geraniums including *Geranium phaeum* 'Album', *G. sylvaticum* 'Album', *G. sanguineum* 'Album', *G. pratense* 'Album', *G. robertianum* 'Album' and *G. r* 'Celtic White', which are directly descended from our wild crane's-bills. This makes a very satisfying native-to-garden plant cross-over in a wilderness garden. Tall clumps of the white-flowered form of goat's rue (*Galega officinalis* 'Alba') and both *Tanacetum balsamita* and feverfew (*T. parthenium*), with their clusters of daisy flowers, were among the original herbs I wove into the borders. Edible herbs included asparagus, white chives and parsley, which, together with the fruits, provided plenty for a browser like me.

GRASSES I mingled ornamental grasses into the herbaceous layer of planting. The grasses help to make the transition to the "garden meadow" and in turn to the traditional hay-meadow beyond. I have always loved grasses and now that they have become fashionable, there are more and more available from nurseries. I am particularly attracted to those closely related to our own native grasses. Garden forms of molinias, carex and deschampsias are very much at home in our garden and the true British native species can be found growing in ancient grassland not far from here. *Molinia caerulea* 'Moorhexe' is descended from our native purple moorgrass with a linear form similar to its parent and dark, pencil-slim flower spikes like exclamation marks. *Deschampsia cespitosa*, our silvery flowered, native hair grass, has cultivars with both bronze and straw-coloured flowers. In addition to the true species, I grow *Deschampsia cespitosa* 'Bronze Veil' and *D.c.* 'Golden Veil' and relate their subtle colours and hazy, misty form to the definitive flower colours and the specific mood of the borders.

Although there are many scented white-flowered shrubs, there are comparatively few fragrant herbaceous plants. *Lupinus* 'Noble Maiden' is an exception, as is *Phlox* 'White Admiral', waiting in the wings to waft its distinctive perfume into the warm summer air.

The field mice and other small furry creatures certainly don't seem to care one bit about the colours or origins of the grasses. I find many of the tussocks have all manner of snug little homes where they have used the softer of the leaf blades to make nests. Birds seem to find the tougher blades of some ornamental grasses to be very enduring nesting material. Insects move into the dense centres of the tufts and tussocks, and I am convinced that grasses earn their place in a wildlife garden. But there is one in particular that I would be unable to resist even if this were not the case. To me, life would be poor indeed without the joy of seeing the golden, oaten flowers and seed-heads of *Stipa gigantea*. Even though it hates my cold, wet winter soil, such is the spellbinding beauty of this grass that I was prepared to make an exception to my non-mollycoddling policy and lift my three young clumps to overwinter in the poly-tunnel for the first year or so until they were well grown and began to be established.

Miscanthuses are imported from North America but we have the moist and fertile conditions they need to thrive here. *Miscanthus sinensis* 'Silberfeder', one of the tallest,

demands plenty of space to make an impact. It has a particularly spectacular winter effect when windblown hither and yon. As with other miscanthus, it produces a soft rustling sound that gives it extra-charismatic garden-worthiness.

BULBS   Once I had studied the colour and characteristics of the plants and monitored the measure of success I could achieve with the herbaceous plant and grass selection, and once the volume of stocks had increased, I started to arrange them into more permanent positions within the framework of the now satisfactorily maturing trees and shrubs. Only then did I gradually start to introduce bulbs.

Most bulbs have a white form but in spite of this I have not been very adventurous with my selection. I am content with drifts of snowdrops, snowflakes, anemones, white narcissus and Star-of-Bethlehem, all of which naturalize easily and provide a sequence of early pollen and nectar for bees and other insects when they hatch or emerge from hibernation. This is the perfect garden for narcissus and snowdrops, which are generally eschewed by creatures foraging for vegetarian food. My assortment of bulbs has so far survived the appetites and annoying habits of the rabbits and squirrels, but the wet winter ground has proved more of an adversary. Of the crocuses I have tried to grow, C. tommasinianus (though not white) is the only one with the tenacity to spread with any conviction. My personal collection of old varieties of narcissus thrive in the borders and the grass of the garden meadow. I love the intoxicating scent of the later-flowering pheasant's eye varieties, especially N. 'Sinopel', with its green-edged corona (instead of the usual cadmium-red one).

The emergence of the first snowdrops is one of the highlights of the gardening calendar. What a perfect bulb for a white wilderness – a flower that is equally at home in woodland, grassland or border. I have collected about half-a-dozen excellent varieties of snowdrops but I have no wish to add many more and become a galloping galanthophile. Our wild Galanthus nivalis is exquisite as it is, without being altered in any way, but the taller, more full-bodied varieties, such as G. elwesii or G. 'Atkinsii', make more of an impact where they have to struggle to peep through the petticoats of shrubby plants or penetrate a dense mat of ground cover.

Beneath the trees and amongst the shrubs, a summer haze of British native and ornamental grasses intermingles with wildflowers and hardy herbaceous plants to create tussocky habitat for insects and small mammals.

WILDFLOWERS IN THE BORDERS A great proportion of the wildflowers we see in the countryside are white. There are also some unusual white forms of wildflowers which I feel honour-bound to nurture. I have white forms of ragged Robin, campion, foxglove, greater knapweed, devil's-bit scabious, self-heal and bugle, most from local sources. All these plants provide vital sustenance for wildlife in exactly the same way as do their coloured relatives. I grow them in both meadows and borders and one or two in the woodland or at its edge. I love to see bumblebees nectaring on the beautiful flowers of white deadnettle (*Lamium* sp.). It has an efficient running root system, so I grow it where it can spread without interfering with other less robust plants.

WILD WHITE UMBELS I can effortlessly indulge my fascination with umbelliferous plants, as there are several natives growing more than willingly in this garden. The exception is pignut, a grassland wildflower that grows in profusion in our cemetery but, for reasons unknown, has so far steadfastly refused to germinate anywhere on my land. This confounds my attempts to help provide habitat for and conserve the Chimney-sweeper moth, which depends on this one species for its survival. Cow parsley and hogweed, my childhood passions, moved in from the hedgerows and are welcome in places but I diligently control the spread of seed to prevent an overwhelming invasion. Of course, the alien giant hogweed is strictly banned. Hemlock and hemlock water dropwort have tried to seduce me with their attractive, nectar-laden umbels, but I have been strong-minded in removing them, two of the most deadly poisonous of our native plants. Corky-fruited water dropwort (a wildflower located in south-west England) is socially acceptable in this respect, being non-toxic, and looks handsome in both the meadow (where it belongs) and in the border, where it has also made itself at home. As it fades in midsummer, along comes the beautiful and beguiling wild carrot which is without exception my favourite plant – umbelliferous or otherwise. It is very attractive to insects, in particular soldier beetles. Wild angelica flowers at about the same time and draws many insects to its nectar bar; a biennial with a preference for wet ground, it has no trouble finding places to seed and re-seed.

Of all the white umbelliferous flowers, the humble wild carrot is the favourite of the soldier beetle, and myself. This exquisite plant thrives in the border or in grass although its capricious nature can sometimes be difficult to manage.

OTHER WHITE WAIFS The starry stitchworts, greater and lesser, grow on hedge banks and grassland respectively but I have allowed, or in some cases encouraged, them to grow near shrubs where they can clamber enchantingly through their lower branches. White mignonette (*Reseda alba*) seeds where it will and if it feels so inclined. I would like to be able to place the pretty spires where they could intermingle attractively with the herbaceous garden plants but they always choose odd and awkward places – usually too close to the border edge. This mignonette has a delicious smell of nectar and is an ace bee-plant so I let it have its way. Ox-eye daisies tend to overwhelm other less lusty plants in the borders. I love them and welcome them but by the end of the summer they have overstepped the mark, so I thin them and plant the extras in the garden meadow, thereby gaining more flower-power for the many species of insects that visit this simple but appealing plant.

CLIMBERS AND TWINERS Among the many woody and herbaceous species in the hedgerow, hedge bindweed, old man's beard, bryony and hop twine or clamber over some sections where the hedge is tall and wide enough to withstand bearing an extra layer of vegetation. The white trumpet flowers of bindweed are every bit as beautiful as the much-cherished morning glories, but it is difficult to appreciate this when they invade the garden borders. Since being filled with wonder by the sight of my first Convolvulus Hawk-moth, I have been probably a little too forgiving of bindweed in some parts of the garden but it can do little harm in a healthy native hedge where the moth can visit and possibly breed on the foliage. Old man's beard, with its translucent, fluffy seed-heads, is also good-looking but possibly even more to be feared as it can become very insistent if allowed free rein. I love bryony for its heart-shaped leaves and strings of red berries, but it is a poisonous plant that must be controlled near stock – and children should be controlled near the bryony!

WILD FLOWERS IN THE LAWNS AND MEADOW The wildflowers that colonize lawns (whether we want them to or not) and those that grow in summer meadows do so because of the way we manage the grass. They almost always do best on poor, infertile soils where there is the minimum competition from vigorous grasses. Some

No place in the garden can compare with the beauty and joys of the New Hay Meadow in June. Clary is the perfect living statue to enhance the pastoral setting.

wildflowers, such as self-heal, medick, dandelion, plantain, daisies, cat's ear, clover, speedwell and trefoil, are well adapted to survive regular beheading by the mower. My land is highly fertile and lies very wet in winter so I struggle to increase the diversity of flowering plants. Daisies grow best in the drier parts and creeping buttercup is in its element. I have begun to overcome this problem by building up some of the paths with rubble to form a cambered track, which is far more wildflower-friendly and I can begin to realize a white, daisy-strewn grass path, which many conventional gardeners regard with disdain. Beside the grass track is my stretch of "garden meadow" and at the juncture between mown and uncut grass I can guarantee to find blackbirds foraging.

The first flowers to light up the meadows are cowslips, bugle, lady's smock, sorrel, ragged Robin, yellow rattle, trefoils and ox-eye daisies, which are soon joined by the golden flower-heads of rough hawk-bit. Corky-fruited water dropwort, which is special to our area and soil type, joins in the throng. Insects breed and increase dramatically during summer and from June onwards. Peter and I sometimes pause for tea and a nap in the meadow, lulled by the "song" of bush crickets and grasshoppers, and the buzz and drone of bees and other insects on the wing. Wildflowers, such as knapweed, betony, yarrow, sneezewort, fleabane, wild carrot and devil's-bit scabious, flower through mid- to late summer, roughly in that sequence. They are all wonderful wildlife plants and the meadow is a constant hive of activity and a total joy to behold.

BIRCH COPSE Our two tiny woodland areas each consist of a few birches and two or three Scots pines that are closely planted within about three yards of each other. To achieve a multi-stemmed effect with the birches, we planted the saplings in groups of two or three. Sometimes it worked and in other cases some trees eventually proved unequal to the contest for survival. If I had been a little more patient and prepared to demonstrate my faith in the coppicing system, I could have planted single trees and then cut them to the base after a few years. They would then, in theory, regenerate with naturally occurring multi-stems.

Even a tiny birch copse, such as ours, makes significant woodland habitat for wildlife. The under-storey of white-flowered scented shrubs, herbaceous plants and bulbs offers a sequence of seasonal attractions in addition to the white-barked trunks.

After the oak (294 species supported) and willow (266), the birch supports the next highest number of species of interdependent fauna. Many birds depend on the insects and caterpillars found in these trees, which are constantly visited – particularly by tits and finches. Families of long-tailed tits are frequent visitors and goldcrests are occasional but delightful ones, which are probably also attracted by the pines (93 species). They are even tinier than the wrens, which also hunt for food in these trees. Birches have rather greedy roots but they are light-leafed and provide an ideal dappled canopy for both native and garden plants. I also chose birches for their splendid white trunks, a striking addition to the winter garden.

The shrubby under-storey is comprised of *Cornus mas*, hollies, cotoneasters, sarcococca and skimmia, which all provide berries, and the last two the bonus of winter and spring fragrance. The herbaceous layer includes a matrix of white forms of ground-covering plants such as early-flowering pulmonarias, lamium, lily-of-the-valley and vincas which supply food for the first bees to emerge. The slightly taller *Helleborus orientalis* (white forms) soon follow and then there are geraniums, Solomon's seal, foxgloves and white forms of campanulas, such as *Campanula latiloba*, *C. lactiflora* and *C. persifolia* to follow. I so love the special summer sound-effects made

by large bumblebees in an apparent tight squeeze in a foxglove flower! *Silene fimbriata* is an unusual and self-sustaining plant whose delicate appearance belies its tenacity.

My previously listed sequences of bulbs perform from spring snowdrops to autumn colchicums. All these plants and bulbs have to fight for their domain in a tangle of honeysuckle and ivy. I rarely have to weed but I do have to be a firm referee. Two plants I was unwise enough to throw into the mêlée were variegated ground-elder (what on earth did I expect?) and woodruff. The latter is a native plant with attractive foliage which is aromatic when cut and dried like hay. It is a competent, galloping ground coverer and will grow in the driest and shadiest of woodland conditions, but it is just too efficient to mingle with a mixed community of plants and it out-competes all its rivals for space.

The proximity of the birch copses to the shrubs and herbaceous plants in the adjacent mixed borders simulates the woodland-edge habitat found in the countryside and again, in conservationist's language, forms the "ecotone zone" where one sort of habitat eases into another. This woodland-edge habitat has the benefit of shelter and gradually increasing light levels. For instance, we often find Speckled Wood butterflies, a woodland species, sunning themselves on shrubs on the southern outskirts of this part of the garden.

SPECIFIC HABITAT BOOSTERS

Mature woodland trees shed debris in the form of leaf litter, twigs and damaged branches, which fall to the ground and feed the fungi, flora and fauna of the woodland floor. It takes years before the trees are mature enough for the system to provide for the opportunist range of life that relies on such an element of apparent disaster. The wildlife gardener often has to improvise to speed up the procedure of habitat creation.

WOODEN STRUCTURES   We have various log-piles around the garden and save some weird and wonderfully shaped branches to make interesting-looking, sculptural arrangements. Dead leaves tend to gather around the larger heaps and add insulation. Some of our configurations of materials have been occupied by hedgehogs or other creatures which seek places to hibernate, hide out or breed. We use wood from a variety of tree species and this helps attract a wide range of fungi

We have positioned varied "eco-heaps" of logs and stones to provide valuable breeding, sheltering, hiding and hibernation sites for insects, reptiles, amphibians and small mammals. Some, like this stag-beetle pile (below), have been customized for specific creatures with their particular requirements.

and insects as the wood biodegrades. Our arrangements of logs are formed into interesting features and attract a wide range of fungi and insects as the materials biodegrade. Some of the logs have been set in the ground (about 45cm/18in deep) to encourage the endangered stag-beetles whose habitat is being seriously eroded.

In the White Garden, our log edging helps to define the woodland paths and retain the chunky bark chippings we use for a dry, weed-free surface. These lengths of wood are just lightly set in the soil and I am always amazed at the mass of insect life which soon colonize the area around them. Log piles are becoming increasingly scarce in our countryside as intensive agriculture requires ever-larger fields and as traditional woodland management has declined.

STONE STRUCTURES Dry-stone walls are also very user-friendly to a great range of wildlife. Unfortunately, there are very few local stone walls in our area of Dorset. We didn't have the resources to build any seriously large walls but we constructed several small "eco-heaps" (as I call them) using recycled flint, limestone and air-bricks from a local demolition job. To increase the biodiversity, some of these features were built in fully exposed, sunny sites and some on the shady woodland edges. Incorporating some logs and turf helped to boost the wildlife-friendliness and to encourage native plants to colonize. There are built-in cavities of various sizes to provide (hopefully) habitat for a range of creatures from insects to reptiles and small mammals – including field mice and hedgehogs. We particularly hope to accommodate slow-worms and toads (good garden pest predators) as well as masonry bees and bumblebees (both excellent pollinators), who like to nest in holes. The latter sometimes move into redundant mouse-holes.

OTHER MATERIALS Apart from wood and stone, there are many materials which, when laid on soil, provide opportunities for creatures to make their homes. If we peer under a sheet of corrugated tin or almost any upturned vessel, we can be certain to find holes and tunnels and sometimes the poor creature which hitherto regarded the dark lid as a bastion of surreptitious and safe habitat. Lengths of plastic, ceramic or metal pipe or tough tubes of cardboard, are used both for passages or underpasses, for living quarters and for storing food. Old boots, whether lodged into a hedge, set into the ground, or thrown casually into any vegetation where they may be overgrown (or even just parked by the back door) are more than likely to be occupied by nesting birds or mice. Each year I look forward to peering into my ever-increasing line-up of boots (such are modern manufacturing methods, they are constantly discarded but not wasted!) while old-fashioned kettles are a classic nesting place for robins.

BIRD- AND BAT-BOXES As well as all the artificial and semi-natural habitat we try to create we also put up a few extra bird- and bat-boxes. Our hedgerows are old and valuable but not so ancient as to provide really deep, safe nesting places for some of the wildlife we would like to attract: woodpeckers, owls, dormice and bats, for instance. In spite of being a protected species, bats are one of our most threatened creatures and need all the help we can give them. In fact, apart from putting up bat-boxes, safeguarding their chosen roosting sites, and encouraging insect life, there is little the amateur can do. In the event of any problems the public must consult the relevant authorities (see page 204). Bats are very sensitive to the smell of humans and their chemicals, so untreated wood must be used for bat-boxes and it is best to buy them from specialist suppliers. Bats appreciate several boxes in close proximity – perhaps three or four around one tree trunk and this increases the chance of attracting them to the garden. Even so, it may take several years and, although we see bats on the wing, I am not convinced we have a result from our fairly recent efforts.

Owl-boxes can be bought custom-made for a particular species of owl. We have erected a large, elongated box type for the tawny owls we know to be resident and a very large "chalet-style" home for the barn owls we hope will take up residence. We were advised to place the barn owl lodgings in a mature oak which overlooks their hunting ground of open grassland on two sides. Our own barn is modern and unlikely to be suitable for owls but it is well used by nesting swallows and wrens. On the east-facing outside wall Peter has built "terraced accommodation" for sparrows, which like communal nesting facilities.

IN CONCLUSION

Over the years, I have been thrilled and amazed as I have carefully observed the visiting wildlife. I have studied both the ecological details and colour discrepancies of a large range of white plants, both woody and herbaceous, and it has been fascinating to see how they interrelate with each other and with the wildlife they support. I shall now allow this garden to be further relaxed and become an even less controlled wilderness. I am not going to harass the borders into containing any plants which are not lion-hearted enough to compete without my mothering and nagging. The less disruption that I cause, the better it is for wildlife. Native plants are of more value to wildlife than most garden plants so, more than ever, I want to learn how to live in peace with my "weeds" and just direct them a little when they take advantage of my leniency. Of course, it may all become so chaotic that one day I could lose my credibility as a gardener and garden-maker, but I can feel satisfied that Peter and I have left few stones unturned in our determination and homespun efforts to help conserve wildlife and wild plants. Certainly, we have valued every minute of the journey along the sometimes smooth and sometimes rocky path of our garden-making during our eighteen years at Sticky Wicket.

GARDEN MANAGEMENT

This chapter outlines the key points in managing a garden to be in "tune with nature". In other words, how to strike a balance between our own needs and those of the different forms of wildlife, large and small, that we must recognize and support.

A generous mulch of home-made compost helps to prevent the need to water, except in extreme conditions.

FUNDAMENTAL REQUISITES for plants are the same as those for humans and animals so these are the guidelines I use for my holistic system of management: a safe environment with enough space, fresh air and light; protection from extreme elements; a well-balanced diet with sufficient uncontaminated water; appropriate hygiene standards and a stress-free treatment with understanding. (This automatically rules out being hit with chemicals or being genetically modified.)

At Sticky Wicket, this amounts to creating the right balance of shelter and shade to safeguard the diversity of plants I have selected to suit my soil type. Young plants receive special attention and protection. We grow plants that will attract beneficial wildlife, such as pest predators, and create suitable habitat for these creatures to feed and breed. Likewise, we include plants that benefit others and help ward off disease.

We do not use chemical fertilizers, herbicides, pesticides or fungicides. Neither do we use peat or peat-based potting composts; we recycle all the by-products from our gardening activities to make our own. Keeping surface water and watercourses uncontaminated, conserving rainwater and soil moisture, and using tap water thriftily, are an important part of our system of management and this goes hand-in-glove with the way we value and care for our soil.

Correctly managed and well-conditioned soil is the foundation for the well-being of the garden so we nurture our soil and treat our land with great respect. The healthy soil then supplies the plants with all the nutrients they need to grow and the stamina to resist disease.

"Be gentle with our earth", we are urged, "and tread lightly upon it". And so we do; both literally and figuratively. We keep off wet, bare earth to avoid compaction and leave it alone when frozen because the soil structure could be harmed. In fact, we try not to tamper with it more than necessary. Incorporating humus will improve the structure, condition, function, nutrient content and vitality of all types of soil and we do this by regularly mulching with homemade compost and, rather than digging it in, we allow the worms to do the work for us.

With the prediction that global warming will create potentially hazardous climate change, gardeners are going to have to work harder at soil-care if our plants are to

Compost heaps in the making are a great resource for wildlife and the resulting product is every bit as valuable. We feed and condition the soil to ensure the plants are robust and disease resistant.

survive the anticipated conditions brought about by this. We already have to deal with prolonged spells of drought and abnormally wet winters. To give our plants the best chance, we have always invested freely in thorough planting preparation and aftercare, which has so far paid handsome dividends. Surface mulching with humus has reduced the impact of major fluctuations in our clay/loam soil structure, but the same is true for every soil type.

COMPOSTING AND FEEDING

A healthy compost heap is composed of a balance of dry, carbon-rich materials and moist, nitrogen-rich materials. There must also be the right balance of air and moisture. A thriving compost heap never smells and materials speedily biodegrade to provide nutrient-rich humus for the garden. Rather than using chemical fertilizers, home-produced compost is a far superior, natural and more environmentally friendly way to nourish the soil and, at the same time, condition it. By composting garden and household vegetable debris we can make a vital contribution to the health of the environment by reducing the load on land-fill sites.

We take great care not to position any compost-making unit where any resulting concentrated effluent can run directly into, and pollute, nearby ground water and watercourses, or leach unwanted nutrients into our wildflower meadows.

Compost heaps can be a valuable source of food and warmth for wildlife. Our heaps are visited by scores of birds, especially in winter when, as well as foraging for a share of my worker-worms, they will also gather to bask in the warmth generated by the invisible army of bacteria and fungi working on the first stages of decomposition. We have to be cautious when moving or turning compost because there is a very real chance we may find a toad lurking there. We also need to take great care not to disturb hedgehogs, which may welcome the drier corners of this habitat for hibernation or breeding. Slow-worms are attracted to compost conditions, which are perfect breeding places for them, where they can rely on the ready food supply of slugs doing what slugs are so well designed to do – processing and disposing of vegetation. Grass snakes sometimes hide and breed in the warmth of the decomposing compost. Admittedly rats are an occasional problem, forcing us to set humane traps.

The advantage of all these tunnelling creatures is that they keep the heaps brilliantly aerated. In this respect there is a plus side to having moles (generally disadvantageous in that they eat massive numbers of the red worms that greatly assist in breaking down the materials). Unless we were to build or buy an efficient, custom-made, vermin-proof compost container, excluding moles is not an option for us. My garden is a gift to wildlife so by imprisoning the compost to exclude moles, I would also deny access to creatures for which a compost heap is a terrific resource for food and habitat. Our recycling system supports beneficial wildlife from tiny organisms to quite large ones! We sometimes have visiting or resident foxes inspecting the heaps for worms, beetles and other tasty morsels.

We create conditions where mixed plant debris can biodegrade efficiently and therefore speedily. When our formula is right, the compost will heat up to about 60 degrees C (140 degrees F) and the first stages of this aerobic decomposition will be rapid. The larger the heap, and the more materials added at one time, the hotter it is likely to get.

NOTE: I am fortunate in having plenty of space to make compost in well-organized heaps on the ground but in a small garden it may be more efficient, tidier and possibly more hygienic to use custom-made containers, where heat and moisture can be more easily regulated and vermin excluded.

OUR COMPOST HEAP RECIPE

DRY (CARBON-RICH) INGREDIENTS These include non-woody hedge clippings, ripped up or crumpled paper and cardboard (not glossy or coloured), straw, wood chippings and some autumn leaves and stalky debris.

WET (NITROGEN-RICH) INGREDIENTS These include lawn clippings, herbaceous excess and dead-headings, suitable weeds, kitchen vegetable waste and some windfall fruit.

ACTIVATORS Comfrey and nettles are excellent compost activators but we take care to add the leaves and flowering stems before they make ripe seeds. We grow comfrey close to the compost area for easy access and regular application. (There are compost activators you can buy from garden centres but make sure they contain only organic substances.)

We are fortunate to have farmyard and stable manure which we add in layers. It is a wonderful bonus to the process and the end-product of composting.

Urine, human or animal, will activate the process of decomposition. If you do not have farm stock or horses, it only requires a little imagination! (Cottage gardeners used to refer to the useful application of "night water"!)

Method

- Include mature stems of herbaceous plants (for example, asters), haulms of peas and beans or clematis stems at the bottom of a new heap to make an airy base (but you may need to chop up very long or thick stems).
- Build the heap up in varied layers of ingredients and avoid an excess of any single material at one time.
- Turn the compost from time to time, mixing the ingredients from sides to middle and letting in air as the layers rise.
- Try to regulate conditions to prevent the compost getting too sodden or dried out but if the ingredients are well balanced and well mixed this is not usually a problem.
- A waterproof covering reduces the amount of nutrients likely to be washed away in winter but needs to be folded back to allow summer rain to moisten the decomposing ingredients.
- It helps if the top of the heap is rounded in winter to deflect excess rainfall and if it has a central depression in summer to capture any summer rain.

Results

After the bacteria and fungi have done their work, the heap cools as worms and other invertebrates continue to process the materials during the anaerobic phase. Within a year the components are transformed into a dark brown, reasonably crumbly, odourless, soil conditioner. A healthy compost heap never smells (ours does only if we have just added a excess of decaying brassica leaves – and then only for a short while.

We use the finest crumbs of this organic matter as potting compost and distribute chunkier material on the borders and vegetable garden as a moisture-retaining mulch and as a soil conditioner, which supplies all the vital, natural nutrients the plants require.

We grow certain crops, such as potatoes, pumpkins and courgettes, on the maturing heaps. Although they rob the compost of a small proportion of their nutrients, they smother any germinating weed seedlings and help the compost to break down during the summer period.

Useful tips
- Do add an occasional forkful of mature compost and/or soil to a fresh heap; it inoculates it with helpful bacteria and fungi.
- Do add chicken and bird droppings as they have a high nitrogen content – we add an occasional bucketful to further stimulate the process of decomposition.
- Do watch out for creatures such as hedgehogs, toads and slow-worms when forking over the heaps.
- Do not add too many grass cuttings: lawn-mowing-overload is the main cause of unhealthy, slimy compost heaps that are slow to break down and start to smell. If there is too high a proportion of grass cuttings at any one moment, mixing in a little straw, dead leaves or paper will keep some airways functioning.
- Do not add too many autumn leaves (especially large, tough ones such as chestnut and plane) as they can "constipate" the procedure. If there is a disproportionate quantity of autumn leaves to dispose of, it is best to stack some of them separately, or place them in bags, where they can be left for a year to break down into valuable leaf-mould.
- Do not include any cooked material or egg shells which might encourage vermin to open heaps.

- Do not include citrus fruit as it can deter worms – we avoid over-burdening the heap with too many skins
- Do not allow weed seeds or roots of pernicious weeds such as bindweed or ground elder. These may survive the digestive process of the decomposing heap and come back to haunt you.
- Do not add faeces of carnivorous pets, such as dogs and cats, to the compost heap.
- Do not site compost heaps close to watercourses; they are an environmental hazard.

ADDITIONAL FEEDING

Well-made compost usually contains all the nutrients a plant needs, although some nitrogen may be leached away if the heap gets too wet. It is sometimes necessary to supplement greedy fruit and vegetable crops or boost the diet of the juvenile, ailing or geriatric plants. An organic fertilizer such as pelleted chicken manure or liquid seaweed would be appropriate but a home-made brew of comfrey and nettle does the trick for most of our plants, with perhaps a dose of Epsom salts if any look a bit jaundiced. I daresay I shall one day be forced to comply with EU regulations controlling the application of any such home-made concoctions, and be required to invest in some expensive product that has been costly and energy-consuming to manufacture and probably prepared and packaged thousands of air miles away. Yarrow, which is so excellent in the composting system, can be used as an infusion containing copper for any plant needing a remedial boost. Our poultry-run pond for ducks and geese becomes fouled with their droppings but our roses thrive on the barrow-loads of watery slurry that we spread during the clearance operations.

MULCHING

This is important for soil improvement, weed suppression and moisture retention, and also provides extra wildlife habitat. Mulches can be sympathetic with nature or, by their own "nature", at odds with our best intentions as concerned conservationists. There are various environmental considerations: composted bark and mushroom compost (which may contain chemicals) need to be well processed or they can be damaging to some plants; gravel is a useful mulch but its extraction drains the dwindling earth's resources; coconut by-products involve many air miles of travel which add to atmospheric pollution.

Old carpet, cardboard and newspapers and magazines have their uses where they can be acceptably disguised but coloured, glossy paper must be rejected because it contains heavy metals that are detrimental to the environment. There are biodegradable fleece or jute mats which are excellent, but the expense and limited lifespan is a consideration. Some of the manufactured horticultural fabrics are acceptable, durable, mould to the soil surface and can be cut to size with clean edges which do not fray. However, woven polypropylene is a nightmare in this respect; when the cut edges are exposed, its strands get caught up in implements, and it can be a formidable environmental hazard to any creature that gets tangled up in it.

Well-rotted farmyard manure and leaf-mould are natural, cheap and effective and there is nothing to beat well-made, homemade compost, which incorporates a wide mixture of components including the aforementioned. We spread most of the compost in spring when the plants are beginning to burst into life and when the ground is moist and preferably warming up, and we avoid such operations when the ground is frozen or waterlogged or later on, when it is dried out. A covering of about 5-8cm (2-3in) is adequate in most places but we set a few barrow-loads in heaps in parts of the borders where a reserve is needed for particularly hungry plants or for soil that needs extra conditioning.

We are careful not to let deep layers of compost smother the base of woody stems (including roses) or put deep layers touching tree trunks as this can cause damage. We apply only the thinnest of layers of the most crumbly materials in places where annual plants are sown or expected to set seed. Generous layers of mulch are helpful to prevent annual weeds becoming a recurring issue. A little of this fine compost is spared for top-dressing odd areas of lawn which need repair and encouragement. We save some compost for topping up during the summer – preferably immediately after a shower. We avoid compost near our meadows or flowering lawns, which need infertile soil. With wildlife in mind, we leave most of our leaf litter and windfalls in situ unless they foul paths or smother grass; it is nature's way of returning organic matter to the soil and the worms help to incorporate this seasonal gift.

I wonder what the ruling will be on placing banana skins near roses? They are full of useful minerals including calcium, magnesium, sulphur, phosphates, sodium and silica; much too good to waste! I even make use of horse hair and at moulting time I spread mats of it around the garden, hoping the soil and plants will benefit from the trace elements it contains.

RECYCLING PRUNINGS

Nothing is ever wasted at Sticky Wicket and, provided it is healthy, every pruned branch, stick or stem is put to use in either a decorative or functional way. With plant welfare in mind, we tackle "the 3Ds" first – removing dead, damaged or diseased material. We prune with the well-being of our wildlife as important a priority as the health and appearance of the plants. When push comes to shove with tricky decisions about the timeliness of a pruning operation, we put the welfare of the wildlife first and are exceptionally careful with hedge-trimming. I ask myself what I am specifically trying to achieve with the pruning. Do I need to control the plant to a manageable size or shape to keep the planting proportions or emphasize a feature of my design? Is it necessary to prune in order to thin, thicken or regenerate stem growth, to stimulate the formation of flower or fruit or to heighten the foliage effect? It isn't a compulsory procedure for every plant every year! Once I have decided my strategy and completed the task, I consider ways to recycle the prunings and benefit nature at the same time.

We prune nearly all our shrubs in winter before birds start to nest, aiming to complete by the end of February but with week one in March an absolute deadline. Walls and hedges and other prime nesting sites are dealt with as a pruning priority and any building repairs (or decoration) also have to be dealt with outside the nesting period. Whatever the conventional wisdom, unless we can be one hundred per cent certain a shrub is unoccupied, summer pruning does not begin until August when the birds have finished nesting.

Substantial branches of pruned or coppiced wood are used for fencing, furniture, eco-heaps or firewood. With

Every part of every plant is returned to the soil one way or another. Recycling is a serious activity at Sticky Wicket but it has its frivolous side!

the single, whippy stems of hazel, willow or cornus prunings, we weave various features for wildlife and use some for simple, woven plant supports. Our "retired" hazel and willow-woven items, along with thorny prunings, are threaded back into our hedgerows to reinforce and shield nesting sites.

We do not use ash for plant supports because some climbing plants recoil from and mysteriously refuse to cling to its wood. Twiggy stems of hazel and hornbeam are useful for supporting plants or laying over bare ground where seeds are sown. I find they help deter cats and at the same time create a microclimate for germinating seedlings.

Some prunings, including prickly ones, are deliberately left in tidy piles in discreet places around the garden. While they are intact and as they later begin to rot, they offer more habitats for the chain of creatures which play an immensely useful and integrated part in the garden ecosystem.

Where possible, fallen wood is allowed to decompose naturally and thus provide welcome habitat for all sorts of creatures. Twenty per cent of Britain's 22,400 insect species are associated with dead wood and moribund trees, according to the RHS. The dead branches that remain on trees are often used for song posts or look-out points for birds so, from the wildlife point of view, they are a bonus.

If we have seriously diseased wood, which might compromise the health of other plants, I burn it in an incinerator and use the potash-rich wood ash, which must be applied immediately or, if stored, kept in a dry place to prevent the nutrient content being rapidly leached away when wet.

My remaining leftover woody debris is shredded and the chunkiest of the resulting wood chips used directly as a path covering and moisture-retaining mulch while the finer grade material is added to the compost heap.

Shredded evergreen material is harmful to worms, so I separate it from the rest and avoid using it as an ingredient of the compost heap.

MANAGING HERBACEOUS BORDERS

The herbaceous parts of my mixed borders contain plants that are extremely useful to wildlife, not only for the pollen and nectar but also for seed-heads and extra habitat. Over-zealous dead-heading and tidying "for tidiness' sake" could remove this bonus resource and make the border far less hospitable to wildlife. Therefore I clear my borders in easy stages between October and March. My "hands off" system is compassionate to the hibernating or active insects and insect larvae, and the birds and small mammals that feed on them. It helps protect my plants, allows the worms to do their stirring work of incorporating decaying vegetation into the soil, and also supplies sporadic and varied materials for my compost heap. On a personal note, we are left with a winter scene that is especially magical on frosty mornings, has plenty of wildlife activity to entertain us and results in less back strain than a massive autumn assault would.

SUMMER PROGRAMME   We dead-head herbaceous plants where the process of doing so will prolong the flowering period or generate a second flush but leave those, such as eupatorium, sedum and lythrum, which flower just once and have fine, upstanding, winter seed-heads that are both handsome and good for wildlife. We remove the seed-heads of some seriously invasive plants, such as saponaria, that we need to restrain. Hefty, arching or fallen stems that interfere with neighbouring plants can be a problem so we thin or remove the most tiresome. Some herbaceous plants – persicaria is an example – soon become unsightly and break down into a slimy condition as their flowers fade, so we use them for compost before they become increasingly unpleasant to look at and handle.

AUTUMN/WINTER PROGRAMME   Week by week in autumn and early winter, I gradually cut down any such faded herbaceous plants once they have nothing left to offer except their tattered remains for recycling.

Rigid, hollow stems provide useful wildlife habitat for insects; I tie these stems in bundles and place them – some vertically and some horizontally – in hedges, among shrubs or in wilderness areas. Less durable and insect-worthy stems are used in compost making (as described).

While vulnerable wildlife retreats or hibernates, late winter is a reasonably safe time to strim some of the areas requiring otherwise back-breaking trimming down.

It is important to prioritize parts of the borders that have vulnerable shoots or spring bulbs emerging among the herbaceous plants.

SPRING PROGRAMME   Ornamental grasses are left undisturbed until late March when they are either trimmed down or combed out depending on the needs of the variety. There is competition for the resulting debris which is either left in situ as a self-mulching material or, if excessive, divided between the compost heap and the wildlife "eco-heaps" for insect life or bird nesting supplies.

Some plants may require restraint or rejuvenation so we lift and divide the plants and replant with pieces of hale and hearty young growth from the edges of the clump. Now is the time to put twiggy hazel stems in place to help prop up the very few herbaceous plants we grow that lack the backbone to be self-supporting.

MANAGING WEEDS

Once we begin to see merit in plants that we perceive as undesirable "weeds", a different light is shone on our battle to restrict our resident native flora in order to enable our introduced garden species to retain their allotted space or to self-seed in bare ground. I take into account the need for discipline but, where practicable I am a little lenient with weeds. British wildflowers are best for British wildlife and crucial for the survival of many species but are unfortunately constantly persecuted in gardens and on farmland. Although I am diligent in controlling weed competition around young plants, I gradually allow certain weeds a restricted place in the border, particularly if they look pretty and offer a suitable colour match to the planting.

However, when it comes to the business of either arbitrating the advance of inoffensive weeds or controlling the invasion of the aggressive ones, identifying species, and understanding their nature, mode of growth and methods of propagation, allows the gardener to stay ahead of the game. Most weeds arrive by seed which may pop, ping, spiral earthwards or just drop fairly locally beside its parent. Some may be spread in bird droppings or even by ants or hitch a lift by clinging to the fur or feather of animals. Other seeds are airborne by virtue of parachute or winged devices or travel even more widely as they float on the wind or on water. The mature plant may rely on an insidious system of self-perpetuation; with creeping roots and stems below the ground or creeping stems and runners above the ground. Roots can be deeply penetrating and stubborn or grow sneakily sideways. Canny as they are, native plants may confound or frustrate us with their combination of survival techniques!

Weeds can adapt their size and even change shape to fit surroundings (however hostile), survive drought, disease or damage and defend themselves with stinging mechanisms, prickly armour or poison. They can produce multiples of thousands of seeds; with a life cycle of seven weeks chickweed, for example, can produce 15,000 million plants a year. No wonder the old adage suggests the conservative estimate that "one year's seeding means seven years' weeding"! Frustrating as all this is for a gardener, I cannot help but admire the doggedness of native plants.

It is six of one and half-a-dozen of another when weighing up the benefits and disadvantages of weeds. On the one hand, they provide for beneficial wildlife and even for the plants we like to grow; on the other, they can overwhelm our garden plants and some can harbour pest insects and diseases. At least I can begin to call the shots and, while I am strict with those that must not become ungovernable, I can be tolerant of those that offer a clear advantage to associated plants and wildlife.

A POSITIVE SIDE TO WEEDS Most weeds have special benefits for the wildlife I hope to attract and can expect to find in my garden: dead nettles, thistles, willowherbs and groundsel are examples and I believe all to have their uses.

Plant cover is important to prevent bare soil baking in hot sun and killing soil life. Weeds are natural ground-cover so, as with all garden "pests", the idea is to control their numbers but not obliterate the ones that have their uses.

Many weeds, such as nettle, colt's-foot and dandelion have herbal virtues from which the garden, my animals and I can benefit. Some weeds – probably more than we think – are edible. They are not all ideally suited to our palate but bittercress, chickweed and young dandelion leaves are very passable in a mixed salad and are highly nutritious. I cook nettles, greater plantain and ground-elder leaves, often mixed with other greens or added to soup.

Some plants have leaves that are a particular asset to, and speed up, the composting process. Nettle, dock, yarrow, dandelion and comfrey have very penetrating or deep tap roots and draw up valuable soil minerals. If the leaves are added to the compost heap, even more enrichment can be speedily returned to our soil and then to our plants.

There are leguminous weeds, such as clover, trefoils and vetches, which manufacture nitrogen in their root nodules and enrich our soil; a bit of a quandary in meadows where they are good for wildlife but can impede the development of other wildflowers; good news in the vegetable garden where nitrogen is useful for crop production.

If a weed is, by definition, a plant out of place, then I certainly have no objection to primroses, campion, sorrel, stitchwort and wild carrot – among many others that take up residence in my garden.

In the spirit of the traditional cottage gardener, I "harvest" our unwanted weeds and recycle them to fuel my compost or feed to the hens to produce eggs or to our goats to turn into milk. I find such natural cycles are most satisfying and offer me very constructive ways to approach what could otherwise be perceived as a chore!

TROUBLE SHOOTING FOR WEEDS

Here are a few issues that require special treatment:

SEED SPREAD Preventing the spread of weed seed is my first line of defence, so we try to stay ahead of the game and restrict germination with layers of mulch. With problem invaders, such as willowherb, we remove the plant or its flower stems before the seeds ripen. We are especially diligent with bittercress, annual meadow grass and chickweed which mature and produce offspring in the blink of an eyelid.

If we fail to deal with the plant before the seed ripens, we grasp and capture the unruly seed-heads (particularly those with an explosive or aeronautical nature) in a black plastic bag, seal it and leave them to decompose a little before disposing of the contents. When approaching and handling fluffy, ripe, seed-heads such as willowherb, it helps to do so after dew or rainfall temporarily cripples the aeronautical mechanisms or to dampen them deliberately to momentarily harness them to their stems and prevent them taking to the air when disturbed.

VEGETATIVE INVASION Brambles are excellent for wildlife but bad for our health and temper when they grow in the borders. Between August and September, we cut them back to prevent them from literally "dropping in" from the hedgerows and their root-forming tips (stolons) from anchoring themselves to begin a new dynasty of plants in unwanted places.

Plants with creeping roots are a menace; creeping thistle is wonderful for butterflies but a torment for farmers and gardeners. I bear this little ditty in mind, and try to act on it:

> "Stub a thistle in May, it will be back next day,
> Stub a thistle in June, it will be back soon,
> Stub a thistle in July, it will surely die."

If we have a problem with underground stems (rhizomes) of couch and ground elder, we smother them with a light-excluding material that is durable enough to be left in place for at least a year (the time it takes to kill them off).

Some weeds, such as ground ivy, creeping buttercup and cinquefoil, have creeping stems (runners) that allow the weed to gain territory when your back is turned, at an alarming rate. We try to dig them out in time to prevent them from advancing.

These, and many other weeds, are often easier to remove at the time when they are throwing most energy into stem growth, and there is a temporary armistice in their determination to anchor their roots in the soil.

Our efficient composting system (see above) ensures that neither "undigested" root remains (nor weed seeds) re-inoculate the soil.

ALTERNATIVE METHODS

Turnips are said to deal with a ground-elder infestation, if grown among it, and marigolds, particularly *Tagetes minuta*, also control this unpopular weed as well as discouraging horsetail and ground ivy. I have had some success with a method whereby you cut the growth of perennial weeds, having allowed them to grow until about to flower, and then lay them thickly on the surface of their own roots. For some reason, and in some cases, it seems to debilitate them.

Flame throwers are useful weed deterrents for certain places, such as paths, but we find we have to persevere with repeated treatments, especially with the highly resistant annual meadow grass. Insects can accidentally frazzle in the inferno so I keep a keen look out for ladybirds and other innocents.

The use of herbicides is understandably condemned by the Soil Association because of the side-effects on soil health and certain creatures (including humans). It clearly makes sense to eliminate unnecessary risk and avoid using them.

POTENTIALLY HAZARDOUS WEEDS One or two weeds are poisonous and I am resolute in preventing the spread of those that might cause a problem in the wider environment: for example, ragwort and hemlock water dropwort could spread onto neighbouring farms.

Alien species can threaten our native wildflowers so I take a responsible stand and assiduously deal with plants such as Himalayan balsam, Japanese knotweed and giant hogweed if any stray my way.

A few weeds can carry pests and diseases that occasionally transfer to crops and ornamentals. I remove every seedling of rape that germinates from bought-in bird seed. There is no way of knowing and no certification to suggest whether or not they are GM-contaminated and I adhere to the precautionary principle and fight tooth and nail to keep my land GM-free until the safety of such plants is proven.

RECYCLING WEEDS   All the inhabitants at Sticky Wicket have to work for their living! This is a cottage garden in essence and our poultry plays an important part in our garden recycling system. They delight to scratch about among the weeds which we dump among the alders and willows. "Civilized" weeds are sacrosanct for our well-ordered compost heap but "uncivilized" ones, with indestructible seeds or pernicious roots, can be reliably dealt with by our chicken army. Few weeds survive in the run, but the ones that do succeed do little harm and are welcome. Weeds, such as bitter-cress and annual meadow grass, can sometimes survive the composting process but not once they have been through the gut of a chicken.

Nettles, docks, buttercups and excessive mint are hard to discard without root re-growth coming back to harass us but it doesn't matter much in here. Delicious, organically produced eggs become the by-product of unwanted or surplus vegetation. The year-round eggs supply feeds family and friends handsomely. By-product eggshells are baked dry, ground up and fed back to the hens as grit, which they need for healthy digestion and efficient egg-production. Some crushed shell is scattered on our vegetable garden to add calcium where brassicas are grown and we might also try using them to discourage slugs – if we had an unsolved problem!

When our duck pond is refreshed, water is spread onto parts of the garden, complete with its sludgy, high-nutrient content. When hen sheds (and dovecote) are cleaned out, the "guano" is added to the compost heap to enrich its nutrient value and help to activate the process of decomposition.

Quite a return on a few pesky weeds!

KEEPING PLANTS HEALTHY

It obviously makes sense to match our choice of plants to soil type and conditions, exposure to wind and sun, and extremes of heat and cold and, in this respect, native plants are easiest to evaluate and accommodate. Drainage is the easiest thing to change if needs must and, although it was necessary for us to deal with some of our ill-drained sites, we have conceded to the nature of our clay-based, loam-topped soil. Our soil pH is neutral, varying slightly across the acres but allowing us a choice of a wide range of native and garden plants. Trying to alter the conditions we are dealt, especially the soil pH is generally far too much of an uphill struggle to be worth attempting.

I bear in mind that most of the garden plants we grow come from far-away places where conditions may be vastly different from our own, so it makes sense to research their origin in order to cater for (or pamper to) their needs. If our climate is to change as dramatically as scientists predict, some doors may close and others may open when it comes to plant choice. I put my money on our British native plants being best able to survive and I seriously hope that, for all our sakes, this will be the case. The highly speculative wisdom of the spread of European imported wildflower species will be sorely tested and debated when such impostors are put to the test. Non-native varieties may have crucial differences, such as flowering times and susceptibility to disease, and even slight differences may be the make or break criteria for survival.

I am fascinated by the sustainable communities of plants where there is a truce in the combat for the supremacy of particularly boisterous species. I study and admire the system in ancient meadows and woodland where an equilibrium exists and, in an optimistic way, I try to emulate this finely tuned type of matrix planting in parts of the garden. I look for plants that will thrive, with roughly matched dynamism, in the conditions I can offer and then I pitch the contenders into contest. I would rather strong-arm a thug than nurture a wimp, but it is as well to recognize the parameters!

AVOIDING PLANT PROBLEMS   I choose both native and garden plants that will eagerly accept our soil type and conditions and the available degree of sunlight and shelter. A study of the natural habitats of our county is fascinating and helpful and, to encourage wildlife, I mimic these natural habitats, such as wetland, grassland, woodland and the ecotones where one habitat meets another.

I use many British native plants, local to my county, and mingle some of them with introduced garden plants. Native or garden plants with fruit, berry, seed, pollen, nectar and larval food plants are a life-line for wildlife. I grow wildflowers from locally sourced seed or buy it from reputable seed merchants that guarantee the seed is of British provenance, not from imported British forms grown abroad.

I try to place garden plants in conditions similar to that of the natural environment of their country of origin.

Discovering how to select and encourage plants to live compatibly in a plant community helps me work towards achieving equilibrium between species. I find it helpful to select ornamental border plants that are reasonably well-matched in terms of gusto for community border life.

Plants are pretty wise at choosing the right place to put themselves so I seldom refuse a volunteer. I generally leave self-seeded plants in place unless very much at odds with my vision for the border or seriously invading another plant's space.

Annuals, the opportunists of the plant world, rapidly make seed to ensure their perpetuation; I try to pre-empt such activities with unwanted species and create suitable conditions for those I would like in their place.

It is important to recognize the pace and tenacity of the spread of ground-covering plants and only introduce the most uncompromising squatters (such as lamium, periwinkle, woodruff and comfrey) where their job is exclusively to exclude other vegetation.

I avoid plants known to be susceptible to disease and avoid monocultures of plant species (such as roses) as this may provoke vulnerability to disease.

COMPANION PLANTING

Although I have excluded our vegetable garden from the main chapters of this book, I grow some edible plants in my flower gardens, too. It is worth noting here that our food crops are organically grown and, while we are not aspiring to be entirely self-sufficient, we have a fair supply of fresh, chemical-free and GM-free vegetables all year round. Nothing compares to the flavour, freshness and overall wholesomeness of organically reared home-grown vegetables so they justify any amount of extra commitment – even digging by moonlight!

Apparently there is insufficient scientific evidence to support ancient folk law and some of the theories of companion planting, but common knowledge and common-sense have underpinned traditional garden husbandry since man began to cultivate land for crops. Certainly there are many plants that have herbal attributes which help us to avoid using environmentally harmful chemicals. Such herbs are usually also excellent nectar plants and will attract pollinating insects that are so vital to the formation of seeds nuts, fruits and berries. Companion planting is dismissed by some sceptics as "old wives' tales". Maybe; but the old wives had a special wisdom and many of their beliefs and practices survived and are applied today, particularly in herbal medicine and biodynamic methods.

I daresay organic growers ("new wives") of the 21st century may have to revise their know-how to cope with the superbugs which have developed since modern chemicals forced Mother Nature to retaliate against the heavy-handed assault she has so far been dealt. I hold on to my firm faith in nature and, because I never underestimate the power and potency of certain plants (or old wives!), I look forward to broadening my knowledge of natural husbandry; my amateur efforts barely scratch the surface of the fascinating principles of biodynamic husbandry, which take organic gardening to a heightened level. Meanwhile, I revel in the delights of mixing and matching my companions with my selected colours in the four gardens I have described. In my vegetable garden I grow hot-coloured companion plants to attract pollinating and pest-predating insects, or sometimes act as a lure to draw pests away from the crops.

GOOD COMPANIONS FOR VEGETABLES AND ORNAMENTALS Many companion plants happen to come in the lively range of red, orange and strong yellow colours, which I eschew in most of my borders and prefer to confine to my vegetable garden. Red and other odd-coloured vegetables suffer fewer pest attacks because they are naturally camouflaged and less recognizable.

The edible red and gold orache act as an attractive, annual, weed-suppressing cover-crop while they grow as seedlings among the rows of veg. We thin (and eat) most of them but leave some to mature before making seeds for the next generation and plenty for the birds. Our tawny-red sunflowers attract bees to help pollinate our scarlet runner beans, which thread their way around them and later offer seeds for our birds. I include additional strong or hot-coloured plants, such as golden rod, rudbeckias, heleniums and fiery crocosmias, which are pollen and nectar-rich and then seed-laden in autumn. Seed-heads are left until February for the birds, which deal with any over-wintering pest insects.

Some herbs, such as the dye plants anthemis tinctoria and woad, and others, such as fennel, achillea and agrimony, have strong yellow colouring and join my throng of plants which have dual benefits to wildlife and organic vegetable production.

Amongst the vegetables I grow a riot of hot-coloured companion plants, including fennel, to attract useful predatory insects and pollinators, such as hoverflies, which help to control pest insects.

Achillea is a good example; it is a good nectar plant with useful seed-heads and its root secretions activate disease resistance in nearby plants. Foxgloves and camomile also stimulate healthy growth of other plants and nettles can profit plants – especially fruit – in the same way.

Plants contain all sorts of natural chemicals to attract pollinators or repel predators away from themselves or their neighbours. For instance, aromatic plants such as tansy and mint contain substances which repel certain insects. Nasturtiums lure Cabbage White caterpillars and black-fly away from brassicas, repel white-fly and woolly aphids, attract hoverflies, are edible and full of vitamin C and iron, and have antiseptic properties. A pretty impressive CV, which can only be eclipsed by the merits of evening primrose. This is well known for its long list of medicinal properties, plus it has edible flower buds and roots and is evening scented to entice night-flying moths. African marigolds are said to emit substances that kill harmful nematodes in soil and are said to be best mates for potatoes and tomatoes.

Caterpillars and aphids edge away from garlic, which can be planted near susceptible plants or applied topically as a liquid dilution. Both garlic and chives have a reputation for their ability to help protect roses from black spot and I am almost convinced the leeks in my borders have the same aptitude.

There are mixed opinions as to the legitimacy of the assertion that caper spurge deters moles. I wonder if it is purely circumstantial that I find relatively little mole activity in my vegetable garden where this herb grows freely.

PEST CONTROL   Chemicals spell disaster to wildlife and must be avoided, so we manage the garden to pre-empt problems from pest, disease or over-bearing weed problems. Encouraging beneficial wildlife helps turn the contest between pest and predator in our favour. We actually need a few of the pest insects to encourage a healthy population of the necessary predators. Less than one per cent of Britain's 22,400 insect species are pests!

If there is an acutely disruptive imbalance I have, on very few occasions, used "applied" biological control in the form of nematodes for pest insects, such as vine weevils and slugs. Naturally-occurring biological control is cheaper and more fun. Birds, bats, hedgehogs, frogs and toads, beetles, ladybirds, lacewings, hoverflies, slow-worms, centipedes and wasps are there to help. Positive thinking also helps; we regard our small number of aphids as "bird and ladybird food" – then they barely bother us! There is always the finger-and-thumb or heavy-boot technique for any particularly disagreeable little blighters.

DISEASE CONTROL It seems that most plants get sick because we invite them to live in inhospitable conditions, so that plight is the first thing to avoid or relieve. Growth-stressed, or otherwise unthrifty, plants are more susceptible to, and less able to deal with secondary problems, such as pest invasion or fungal attack.

My first line of defence is to watch out for pointers: changes in colour are often the first clue and can indicate that physiological problems, such as drought, water-logging, wind-rock and scorching or nutrient deficiency, may be the cause. If it is a bacterial or viral infection I don't know of any effective weapons to treat contaminated plants. Fungal infections are often too far gone to remedy unless identified and treated with great expediency. Certain fungicides – such as sulphur and Bordeaux powder – are permitted by the Soil Association but we never use them as, all too often, products certified as "safe" are withdrawn from the shelves.

We prefer to cut out the affected parts of the plant and give them the TLC needed to help them recover. Mostly they do. If the problem is widespread, I believe it unlikely that chemicals will successfully control a runaway disease. My plants either eventually survive the problem or they don't – *c'est la vie*. With contagious diseases such as potato-blight, fire-blight and some viruses, we are scrupulous in removing and burning all affected plant material immediately.

PROPHYLACTIC AND ORGANIC TREATMENT The three Ds – damaged, diseased or dead wood – are removed and incinerated if contagious. It is vital to disinfect secateurs after cutting into diseased wood but ideally the pruning cuts should be made well below the infected stem or branch so that the tools remain uncontaminated and the plant will recover from a healthy growing point.

Lacewing and ladybird houses provide additional habitat for these hugely beneficial aphid predators.

Morning glory (*Ipomea* sp.) and poached egg flower (*Limnanthes douglasii*) are among favourite plants for hoverflies, whose larvae have a voracious appetite for aphid larvae.

We feed and encourage the birds such as tits, which help control pest insects, robins, which eat vine weevil larvae, and thrushes, which hammer away at the snail population. Frogs and toads hop about in pursuit of slugs while hedgehogs and slow-worms are also useful predators.

The use of slug pellets is obviously out of the question and is thankfully unnecessary in our garden. Only rarely have I needed to use commercially produced nematodes as an additional biological control for abnormally increased populations of slugs in the vegetable garden or for infestations of vine weevil amongst the ornamentals.

A rather more tangible method is to capture the enemy. I do my own share of predation and go out at night and squash a few undesirables (such as the aforementioned). I sometimes trap slugs in citrus fruit skins and vine weevils in rolls of corrugated paper. I find beer traps attract other boozy creatures that I have no wish to drown. Slugs find it hard to resist an up-turned bucket that has contained a bran and milk mixture so they offer me a transparent clue to making a trap with these ingredients. Soot, crushed egg shells and coffee grounds are also recommended for slug control.

I keep meaning to try using moth-balls to deter carrot-fly, but sowing them thinly with spring onions alongside works fairly well in disguising the scent which attracts this pest insect and this is a more natural form of deception.

Natural pest and disease deterrents made from plants and materials, such as horsetail, rhubarb, elder, garlic, tobacco, soap and soda, were tools available to our ancestors and no doubt served them well. Although the use of home-made concoctions is now outside the EU law, I doubt if such an embargo is enforceable.

MANAGING HEDGES

Species-rich hedgerows with British native plants are superb for wildlife and, whether they are regularly trimmed or allowed to grow tall, they serve an abundance of different creatures in different ways. The thicker the hedge the better, and an A-shape grows most successfully, but the most important thing is that they are not interfered with between March and August when birds are nesting. It is an offence under Section 1 of the 1981 Wildlife and Countryside Act to intentionally take, damage or destroy the nest of any wild bird while it is in use or being built so I cannot imagine why it is within the law and yet outside the limits of common-sense to even consider cutting native hedgerows between March and August. Birds sing to claim their domain so when I hear them in full voice in February, I make sure all my hedgerow management is very soon up to speed for at least the next six months. In fact, I wouldn't touch them until late December when nearly all the berries have disappeared and the insects have had plenty of time to breed on the leaves. Some of our stretches of hedgerow are cut and laid, or even coppiced, to thicken them up and keep them rejuvenated but this is only likely to happen every ten years or so. Other parts of our hedgerow are trimmed by hand or mechanically depending on the sensitivity of their nature or position.

It is a bit more difficult to be as decisive with garden hedges that are also used for habitat and, depending on choice of species, may also provide food for wildlife, but need to be shaped and controlled if they are to fulfil their structural or decorative function. Just one false snip and the cover can be totally blown for a nesting bird even if no harm appears to have been done, so I carefully consider the nature of each of my garden hedges. The hornbeam hedge that shelters my vegetable garden is a well-used haven where birds regularly nest in the gnarled framework beneath the annual growth it produces in a year. Fortunately for the birds I allow it to remain untouched until August.

My mixed box (*Buxus sempervirens*) and privet (*Lonicera nitida*) hedge is also routinely used as a nesting place and I am faced with a dilemma when it makes a massive amount of bushy growth and needs cutting in prime-time May and June. The exterior fuzz of young shoots augment the natural wildlife cover of the woody interior but cause the hedge to become an increasingly shapeless feature of the design of the garden. I must either accept the disordered appearance, and give such hedges an annual winter chop (which can be a bit savage for some species) or lightly trim those with the absolute regularity required to keep the profile as unaltered as possible.

My approach with hedges depends on the species of plant, the probability of its occupation by vulnerable wildlife and whether or not I can very discreetly peer into the branches and detect any occupied sites. While gardening in summer months I leave a wide birth around any known nesting sites.

HEDGEROWS   I have my own special procedure when it comes to boundary hedgerow management.

During December and January I cut out sticks for peas and any whippy hazel stems I may need for weaving or plant supports. Ash usually makes vigorous growth and the stems are excellent for shredding so the most substantial branches are harvested for this along with the shorter but twiggier field maple and other non-thorny, woody stems with some substance.

Major stems of thorny hawthorn and blackthorn are cut out and set aside in small heaps until the work is complete. The remainder of the hedge is then cut with a hand-held, or tractor-mounted, mechanical hedge cutter. The thorny stems are afterwards threaded back into any gaps in the hedge and some are flattened onto the hedge top where spring growth soon forges through this extra lid of protective covering. This considerably reinforces the hedge's natural defences against predators such as magpies and squirrels and is also effective against human intruders forcing an entrance or domestic pets or stock making an escape. Badger and fox runs are easy to spot and I avoid blocking their passage. As the cut branches gradually biodegrade, they enhance the habitat for insects and fungi and their remains mulch the hedge bottom.

During the summer, long wandering stems of brambles begin their quest to stray into new territory. After the August bird-nesting watershed, I trim and re-trim these where it is necessary to keep them at bay and to encourage fruiting stems for the following year.

If parts of our hedge are to be cut and laid, we also do this in the midwinter period although it is less likely the re-formed hedge will be used for nesting in the first year of its resurgence. Cutting and laying is a traditional countryside practice that involves severing about nine-tenths of the hedgerow trunk or stem and laying it more or less horizontally with just this fraction of its woody lifeline attached. New and vigorous growth occurs along the length of the recumbent wood and large gaps in the hedge can thus be filled.

It may appear to be a radical attack, but the benefits are soon realized and improve and prolong the life of the hedge. If it is well-managed in subsequent years, and trimmed annually to an A-shape, the wondrously rejuvenated hedge will thrive and thicken and its potential for harbouring wildlife will be many times greater than one that is skinny or gappy.

The practice of coppicing a hedgerow (cutting the stems to within a few inches of the base) may appear even more extreme, but is another way of rejuvenating and thickening a hedge, provided it is reasonably healthy and was not too gappy in the first place.

GARDEN HEDGES From May until the end of July, I keep formally shaped and dynamically growing hedges, such as privet, regularly but very lightly trimmed to maintain some order whilst minimizing the risk of exposing nesting sites close to the surface of the thatch of growth. I re-discipline the shape in August and September, allowing plenty of time for the soft regrowth to harden up properly before winter.

I leave less formally shaped and open-branched ornamental hedges, such as philadelphus or forsythia, untouched until after nesting time unless the odd wayward stem can be trimmed with the total certainty that no harm can be done to the resident wildlife.

My living, willow-woven hedge is rewoven during the winter when I conceal my "retired" woven bird features (feeding globes and roosters) among the network of newly threaded stems for extra wildlife cover. The next generation of long wands of new growth are left to grow freely during the summer.

In selected parts of my hedges I weave dense, living, leafy domes by bending and weaving the flexible young stems of hedging plants, such as hazel, willow, cornus and snowberry. If I have sussed out an appropriate place, I am seldom disappointed when, come the autumn, I check for evidence that some of our birds have nested there.

I trim the sides of my hornbeam hedge in August and trim the lengthy top-growth back hard in winter, saving the substantial twiggy stems from the prunings for brushwood for plant supports and tightly bundling the remainder to make additional habitat boosters.

MANAGING GRASSLAND

For the organic and wildlife gardener, the rules of grassland management are very much at odds with the sort of lawn care now the norm in conventional gardens. Our aim is to reduce the fertility level and restrain the over-zealous growth of grass in order to encourage the wildflowers to gain a stronghold. This may be an anathema to some gardeners, who may perceive such broad-leaved plants as "weeds" when they occur in the grass they are trying very hard to encourage, but at Sticky Wicket we see a grassy space as a place where at least some of our much-persecuted wildflowers, and associated wildlife, can be given respite from the environmental maltreatment which is sadly a part of the production of many a "bowling green" lawn.

A chemical-free grass sward is an excellent breeding ground for invertebrates and in turn becomes feeding ground for the birds that forage for these worms, grubs and bugs. We certainly have stretches of luxuriant, verdant lawns but ours are self-fed with the content of white clover that volunteers to grow there and which manufactures natural nitrogen, leaving us with no need, and certainly no desire, to use chemicals.

We have successfully created opportunities for growing wildflowers in damp clay and on nutrient-deprived chalk and rubble and gravel mounds and most of these grassland projects are just a few meters square. We have even succeeded in meeting the ultimate challenge of growing wildflowers in our rich loam of the garden but success did not come without a considerable amount of remedial work.

These grassland patches are cut between one and four times a year depending on the requirements of individual systems. Our one-and-a-half acres of lowland clay meadows are annually cut for hay using traditional methods but with extra proviso that the timing of any such cutting operations are carefully geared to the well-being of the wildflowers and to the welfare of the various associated wildlife. We use a "patchwork" system whereby different sections are cut at different times according to the best interests of both flora and fauna.

The reduced number of mowing operations involved in our overall grassland management has the additional benefit that it lessens the volume of noise pollution and fuel emissions generated from our four to five acres. The cut meadow-grass and lawn mowings are variously either recycled via the composting system, used as a green mulch or fed to our poultry or goats and "returned" to us in the form of eggs and milk.

MANAGING LAWNS
In line with organic principles and for the protection of wildlife, our lawns and grass paths are obviously chemical-free.

With wildlife in mind, we allow, or indeed encourage, mowable wildflowers (or weeds) such as white clover, selfheal, daisies and trefoil, to grow in the grass. To protect insects and help minimize the effects of drought, we never mow our lawns too closely. Where the ground is very compacted I might aerate the turf with a fork in spring or autumn. Where there are muddy patches or there is undue wear, I reinforce with gravelly soil – recycled from our path-weeding operations.

Once a year I re-define all the lawn edges with a spade or half-moon edger. I use these off-cuts of turf to repair subsidence in the lawn or grass paths or where they are mole-damaged.

I harvest wildflower seed throughout the summer and sprinkle the turf with this after their final cut in autumn. I add extra grass seed where I need to cater for the wear and tear on the well-worn routes.

As far as possible I keep off the lawns in winter when they are very wet or frosted.

Some areas are spared the mower blades for some weeks during the summer so that the low-growing flowers can hold their heads a little higher and bloom for longer, as a gift to wildlife.

Our mixtures of fine-leaved, native grasses are less competitive than ryegrass which is great for rugby pitches but would be far too headstrong in this situation and must be avoided where wildflowers are the priority.

Prior to mowing, I painstakingly check the longer grass of flowering lawns for hedgehogs, frogs, toads and newts ahead of the lawn mower or strimmer.

Sometimes I am delighted to find ant hills forming in longer grass. I am careful to avoid scalping them and allow them to eventually form a raised wildflower micro-environment and provide food for green woodpeckers.

MANAGING WILDFLOWER MEADOWS

For the sake of both wildflowers and wildlife, we cut our meadows section by section in a "patchwork" system between July and October. Over-fertile places are targeted first to help reduce the vigour of course grasses. We avoid cutting the more flowery patches until the plants have set seed and thousands of insects have benefited from the nectar-rich plants.

We leave the cut grass in swaths for a couple of days for creepy-crawlies to creep and crawl to safety and for wildflower seeds to shed or be harvested. Careful removal of hay, or cut grass or debris, will avoid a build-up of excess fertility from decomposing vegetation. We leave designated areas uncut and undisturbed for wildlife but the size and position of these is varied from year to year to avoid encouraging coarse grasses or scrub regeneration.

Fertilizers, especially chemical ones, are the enemy of wildflowers so we avoid using any and hope that none will leach onto our land from boundary watercourses.

MANAGING PONDS

It is essential to try and create a balanced environment with the right management and appropriate choice of plant material. As with meadows, excessive nutrients, especially those that are chemical-based, are likely to cause problems, creating similarly excessive or unwanted vegetation. Ponds with too few plants, especially oxygenating ones, will have problems with excess algae (plants with fine filaments that restrict the growth of other plants), which can turn the water green and reduce the oxygen levels crucial to the health of pond water and pond-life. A submersible pump helps to aerate the water while water snails help balance the weed growth.

We have to be aware of and bear in mind the struggle for supremacy between species of aquatic plants and the similar battle for survival between aquatic creatures. We also have to understand that the interrelationship between aquatic flora and fauna can amount to a fragile coexistence. Minimum interference is recommended so that a natural balance can develop, but garden ponds seldom reach an equilibrium that pleases all parties concerned, including the gardener.

If interfere we must, there is never an ideal time to do so as far as wildlife are concerned, but the period between August and October is said to be the most acceptable. When it comes to keeping the pond topped up, rainwater is much healthier than tap water and, in spite of the atmospheric pollutants it picks up, it is hopefully less chemically enhanced than most tap water. Spring-fed ponds are a pure source but might induce mineral-rich water, the cause of blanketweed, which smothers other plants until the oxygenating plants consume the minerals.

I have selected mostly native plants in the hope that they will form a reasonably stable community and encourage pond-life, such as water snails and tadpoles; these consume decaying plant matter and algal growth. Water temperature affects pond-life as well and the idea, as with most other environments, is to avoid extremes. Warm water encourages algae. Deeper water at the centre of the pond helps to regulate temperature fluctuations, as does controlling the amount of plant cover.

We mow our meadows between July and October using a patchwork system of cutting, targeting the most fertile grassy areas first and leaving flower-rich patches to set seed and provide for wildlife.

POND CARE PROGRAMME

Unless absolutely essential we resist the temptation to interfere with the wildlife ponds. If absolutely necessary, we wade in and remove excess vegetation between August and October; underwater plants also require some light for photosynthesis, so we need to see fair play between submerged, floating and emergent plants.

We leave the cleared vegetation beside the pond for two or three days so accidentally displaced creatures can escape before debris is removed to the compost heap. During this time we turn and inspect the debris because some of the weird and wonderful pond-dwellers get trapped among the plants or blanketweed and need to be released back into the water. I am cautious when handling diving beetles and water-boatmen, however, which can deal a mean nip!

We try to relieve the pond of at least some of the fallen autumn leaves to prevent oxygen being removed as they decompose.

February and March is courting and mating time for frogs, with toads usually a couple of weeks behind. They like privacy, so this is the time to steer clear of the pond edge, and just watch and listen from a polite distance.

We take great care when mowing or strimming near the pond, ensuring all visible creatures are chased away and no grass is dropped into the pond to compound the debris situation.

In summer we try to channel in as much rain water as possible to keep the water refreshed and the level constant.

If we do need to use tap water we trickle it in gently to avoid disturbing the mud or sprinkle it on to help with aeration and lower the water temperature.

Movement of water via winter excess rainfall removes salts and toxic materials.

We wrap netting around our submersible pump to prevent blanketweed blocking its filter and mechanism, and we bring the whole apparatus in before the frogs start to hibernate in the deep water in winter.

POND TROUBLE-SHOOTING

- If the pond is heavily frozen over in winter, keep an airway open to allow accumulated gases to escape lest they poison the wildlife. A pond-heater is a good way to keep an opening without trauma to the wildlife but a simple bowl of hot water can be used instead.
- If aphids become a problem on pond plants, I am advised that hosing these insects

into the water provides a snack for the pond creatures and is a positive resolution to the problem.

- Use barley straw to help control blanketweed (but EU regulations may present future obstructions to the way we mange our water). Organically grown straw would be preferable to conventional, potentially contaminated straw.
- If you find a luxuriant green lid of duckweed, gently sift some out with a net or rake (we feed ours to our ducks). It will inevitably re-grow but regular thinning allows at least a little necessary light to penetrate the water and reach the submerged plants.

PROPAGATION

I need to propagate a certain number of plants to keep the garden revitalized or to experiment with new ones grown from seed. Rather than have too many plants imprisoned in pots, I find seeds, cuttings and bare-rooted plantlets are a more environmentally sensitive way to share plants with other gardeners.

Large-scale removal of peat from bogs is annihilating our most precious habitats. Centuries of peat formation have been sacrificed to supply the horticultural trade. Fortunately, enlightened gardeners can now buy peat alternatives or use homemade compost. I insist on using organic, peat-free compost for both sowing and potting on in spite of the fact that seed germination is a bit erratic with some products. Some wildflower seeds prefer to grow in molehill soil, but this inevitably contains other seeds which may need to be weeded out.

SEED-SAVING AND SOWING I harvest seed when it is ripe, in dry weather. As a general rule of thumb, most seeds are ripe when they are hard, dark-coloured and part fairly willingly from their seed-head or capsule.

Seed-heads are then dried in paper bags in the poly tunnel or kitchen. The seed is cleanly separated from the husks and overwintered in paper envelopes placed in waterproof containers in the fridge.

Some seed must be sown when freshly harvested even though the seeds may not germinate until the following spring (or even longer after sowing).

For seeds that are slow to germinate, a covering of grit or vermiculite (for surface-sown seeds needing light to germinate) helps to keep growing conditions healthy.

I sow very few spring-grown plants until the natural growing season begins in March, so only a tiny minority need to be "nannied" in an electrically heated propagating unit. Hundreds of seedlings volunteer in the gravel paths and we carefully lift these and pot all we need.

I try to follow the principles of sowing seed and transplanting plants with the waxing rather than waning moon, out of respect for the fact that the lunar rhythms of the earth's magnetic field affect plant growth, but it is difficult enough keeping up to date with the work, let alone conceding to further limitations.

HERBACEOUS PLANTS   I lift and divide herbaceous plants in spring when the weather starts to warm up and there are signs of growth. I use only the most virile, healthy pieces of plant material in the minimum-sized pot needed to comfortably contain the required length and volume of roots. For these plants I use the most friable of my home-produced compost, topped up with just an inch of so of the more sterile commercial product to minimize weed germination.

I have some shaded benches for juvenile or recently potted plants that need respite from bright sunshine.

I allow about an inch of space at the top of the pots for efficient use of water.

I re-use pots and seed trays, disinfecting any which have traces of diseased plants or very stale soil.

Any woody cuttings I need are done by a friend, Rose Dennison, as she succeeds where I fail.

IN CONCLUSION

Our five acres of garden and meadows undeniably require hard work and dedication. I am not about to claim that everything in the garden is always rosy but I do know for sure that the balance of nature generally swings in our favour. Rabbits, for instance, do very little to endear themselves to us but the unlucky few that end up in a pot make a wholesome dinner. We do suffer the effects of certain fungal diseases, which can blight the look of some of the plants, but in fact most of them survive.

We lose more plants as a result of the increasing wet winters than for any other reason, so we just have to make do with the ones that can cope. Slugs, snails and aphids are the least of our problems and although I get a bit miffed when the mice eat my vegetable seeds, I lose very little sleep over the effects of pests on our plants.

I admit to sometimes feeling a little overwhelmed by certain of the pesky and persistent weeds that I try hard to love and tolerate. But that slight pressure and a few creaking bones are a very small price to pay for living in a flourishing wildlife paradise which is delightfully easy on the eye and which provides essential food for both body and soul.

Our garden flourishes because we work in tune with nature and respect and nurture the soil. Our methods enable us to garden without the use of any chemical fertilizers or pest control, make full use of our weeds and prunings, minimize the need to water and to live in peace and harmony with our wildlife.

USEFUL ADDRESSES

Emorsgate Seeds
Limes Farm, Tilney All Saints
King's Lynn, Norfolk PE34 4RT
01553 829028
(specifies county of origin)
www.wildseeds.co.uk

Suffolk Herbs
Monks Farm, Coggeshall Road
Kelvedon, Colchester, Essex CO5 9PG
01376 572456
www.suffolkherbs.com

G. and J.E. Peacock
Kingsfield Conservation Nursery
Broadenham Lane, Winsham
Chard, Somerset TA20 4JF
01460 30070

Green Farm Plants
Bury Court, Bentley
Farnham, Surrey GU10 5LZ
01420 23202

Nori and Sandra Pope
Hadspen Garden and Nursery
Castle Cary, Somerset BA7 7NG
01749 813707
www.hadspengarden.co.uk

Ian and Angela Winfield
Snape Cottage
Chaffeymoor Hill, Bourton, Dorset
01747 840330
www.snapestakes.com

Knoll Gardens
Hampreston, Wimborne
Dorset BH21 7ND
01202 873931
www.knollgardens.co.uk

The Woodland Trust
Autumn Park, Dysart Road
Grantham, Lincolnshire NG31 6LL
01476 581111
www.woodland-trust.org.uk

Butterfly Conservation
Manor Yard, East Lulworth,
Wareham, Dorset BH20 5QP
0870 7744309
www.butterfly-conservation.org

Bat Conservation Trust
Unit 2, 15 Cloisters House
8 Battersea Park Road, London SW8 4BG
020 7627 2629
www.bats.org.uk

The Mammal Society
2B Inchworth Street, London SW11 3EP
020 7350 2200
www.abdn.ac.uk

Royal Entomological Society
41 Queens Gate, London SW7 4HU
020 7584 8361
www.royensoc.co.uk

Royal Society for the Protection of Birds
The Lodge, Sandy,
Bedfordshire SG19 2DL
01767 680551
www.rspb.org.uk/

The British Trust for Ornithology
The Nunnery, Thetford, Norfolk, P24 2PU
01842 750050
www.bto.org/

C. J. Wildbird Foods
The Rea, Upton Magna
Shrewsbury SY4 4UR
01743 709545 and 0800 731 2820
www.birdfood.co.uk

Flora-For-Fauna
c/o The Natural History Museum,
Cromwell Road, South Kensington,
London SW7 5BD
020 7942 5000
Postcode Plants Database: www.nhm.ac.uk/
science/projects/fff/Tech.htm

The Wildlife Trusts
The Kiln, Waterside, Mather Road,
Newark NG24 1WT
0870 036 7711

Royal Horticultural Society
Vincent Square, London SW1P 2PE
020 7834 4333

Plantlife International
14 Rollestone Street, Salisbury
Wilts SP1 1DX
01722 372730
www.plantlife.org.uk

The Centre for Alternative Technology
Machynlleth, Powys, SY20 9AZ
01654 702400
www.cat.org.uk

The Henry Doubleday Research Association
Ryton Organic Gardens, Ryton on Dunsmore
Coventry, CV8 3LG
024 7630 3517
www.hdra.org.uk

The Soil Association
40-56 Victoria Street, Bristol BS1 6BY
www.soilassociation.org

USEFUL BOOKS

Chris Baines, *How to Make A Wildlife
Garden*, Frances Lincoln Ltd, 2000
Ron Wilson, *Gardening for Wildlife*,
Capall Bann Publishing, 1997
Robert Burton, *New Birdfeeder Handbook*
(RSPB), Dorling Kindersley, 2000
Peter Harper, *The Natural Garden Book*,
Gaia Books Limited, 1994
Charlie Ryrie, *The 'Daily Telegraph' Wildlife
Gardening*, Cassell Illustrated, 2003
Anna Kruger (Editor), *HDRA:
Encyclopedia of Organic Gardening*,
Dorling Kindersley, 2005
Pauline Pears and Sue Stickland,
*Organic Gardening (RHS Encyclopedia and
Practical Gardening)*, Mitchell Beazley,
1999
Bob Flowerdew, *Bob Flowerdew's Organic
Bible*, Kyle Cathie Ltd, 2003

INDEX

ACKNOWLEDGMENTS

Without Peter's love, strength and ingenuity, Sticky Wicket garden would be merely a castle in the air and if it had not been for the support of our family and friends we would have been unable to realize so many of our dreams and aspirations.

Our love and eternal thanks to: our outstanding project team – Emma Munday, Mark Smith and Marcus Lewis; our skilled gardening team – Fizz Lewis and Shane Seaman; Rose Dennison, Theodora Scutt and Ginny Bulman who have propagated so many of our plants; the multi-talented Ed Brooks for a memorable year as a student here and James Duell, Josefina Prieto and Catalina Phillips, who also studied with us, loved the garden and made unique contributions; our very special friends Lorely and Mike Brimson, Nori and Sandra Pope, John and Margaret Sutor, Ian and Angela Whinfield, and David and Marion Brookes for their phenomenal inspiration, love and support.

We could never have survived and opened the garden to the public for sixteen years without the unfailing help and love of my mother, Pauline Wilkes, my aunt and uncle, Pam and Alan Bartlett, my cousin Louise Skett, and our dear Lillian White, who must have baked more than a thousand cakes. Our thanks to Jill Pearce, May and Goff Corke, Carol Wilson, Brian and Sylvia Dicker and other helpers from Butterfly Conservation, plus many others who have volunteered their services for the NGS and other charity open days. But for the praise and encouragement of faithful garden visitors and friends, including Clive Farrell, Dennis and Peggy Seaward, Nigel and Lesley Slight, Sue and Hanna Smithies, and John and Lizzie Leach, we might have faltered over the years.

I thank my genius friend Andrew Lawson for his brilliant photographs of the garden, spanning sixteen years, and Susan Berry for her encouragement and help with this book. I also thank Alison and Ruth Martin, who assisted me with my writing and, along with all those I have mentioned, held my hand through the harrowing time of Peter's illness and in the dark days since his death in June 2004.